CRITICAL ESSAYS IN MODERN LITERATURE

OTHER CRITICAL ESSAYS

ENTRANCES TO DYLAN THOMAS' POETRY

ENTRANCES
TO
DYLAN THOMAS'
POETRY

By RALPH MAUD

University of Pittsburgh Press

Acknowledgment

PARTS OF THIS BOOK have appeared in different form in *Essays in Criticism, Audience, The Explicator, Explorations, Modern Language Notes, Western Humanities Review, English Studies, PMLA,* and *Poesia e Critica.*

I am indebted to the Estate of Dylan Thomas and David Higham Associates Ltd. for permission to quote from Dylan Thomas' writings; to J. M. Dent and Sons, and to New Directions, for permission to use copyrighted poems; to the late Charles D. Abbott of the Lockwood Library and to Oscar A. Silverman, Director of Libraries, State University of New York at Buffalo, for permission to use and quote from Dylan Thomas' notebooks; to Oscar Williams and to William A. Jackson for like permission with respect to holdings in the Houghton Library of Harvard University; to Professor Harry Levin and to Professor Reuben Brower, for their interest over a long period; to the American Council of Learned Societies for a Grant-in-Aid, and to the Committee on Allocation of Research Funds, State University of New York at Buffalo, for several awards; for specific help in research to Ralph Abercrombie,

Julian Abercrombie, Luigi Berti, John Malcolm Brinnin, Edith Capon, Eric Capon, A. C. Cawley, Douglas Cleverdon, J. Howell Daniels, John Davenport, Aneirin Talfan Davies, John Selwyn Davies, Pennar Davies, W. Emlyn Davies, S. W. Dawson, Bonamy Dobrée, William Empson, Meredydd Evans, Doris Fulleylove, Randolph Fulleylove, William Griffiths, Geoffrey Grigson, T. E. Hanley, Rayner Heppenstall, Trevor Hughes, Richard Hughes, Edmund Ions, M. E. James, Alfred Janes, Glyn Jones, Mervyn Levy, Robert MacGregor, Richard Ohmann, Cecil Price, Keidrych Rhys, John Rolph, Ethel Ross, Roberto Sanesi, Pamela Snow, Thomas Taig, Wynford Vaughan Thomas, A. E. Trick, Donald Tritschler, Vernon Watkins, Shirley Whyte, Oscar Williams, Ralph Wishart; and to S. B. and M. P. Jones, first parents of this book.

Ralph Maud
Buffalo, New York

Contents

Chapter 1

Introduction

*"The wisest of the Ancients consider'd what
is not too Explicit as the fittest for Instruc-
tion, because it rouzes the faculties to act."*

William Blake to the
Rev. Dr. Trusler (1799)

THERE IS A PHOTOGRAPH OF DYLAN THOMAS in his Chelsea flat in 1945, his thirtieth year and the poems of *Deaths and Entrances* behind him. The photographer caught him in a brooding mood, his coat and waistcoat unbuttoned, his left hand deep in his coat pocket.[1] He is set amidst the icons of his life. The glass in his hand is almost empty; a quart Guinness bottle stands on the table. Caitlin Thomas is there. In the background are a couple of hundred books in bookshelves (one can make out Whitman and Coleridge in the Nonesuch editions). And pinned to the wall are cuttings of landscapes — Welsh landscapes, who can doubt it? Looking at this scene now, through glass darkened by almost twenty years, we see a surrealist picture, certain of these symbols grotesquely swollen. The beer bottle, which the young hero of *Adventures in the Skin Trade* stuck on his finger, is now huge out of all proportion. Caitlin Thomas has made her own large gesture in *Leftover Life to Kill*, proving that Dylan was worth ten other men. (One has to endure the disappointment of finding in

1

Thomas' own work no divan or bedroom scene: sex is always too close to birth and death to be salacious.) As for the Welsh landscapes, we can safely say that Thomas had never the Welshness in life that has been granted him in death. These three symbols — Drink, Sex, and Wales — are magnified now to the extent that Thomas is disappearing behind them. The Welsh furor of mourning, for instance, has permanently alienated several younger critics in England. But Dylan Thomas was not a "Welsh bard"; he was an English poet. And most of his poetry was written when the three icons were not monstrous, when they comfortably had their place, as in the reassuring Chelsea photograph.

Thomas' bookshelves are still to be mentioned. Unlike the other icons, the poet's books had no part in his fatal celebrity. No one has suggested that he read himself to death. But he did read, and must have read rapidly in early youth to achieve his precocious vocabulary. The opportunity was there in his father's study. In a radio interview the poet's mother has explained how embarrassing it was to his father, the Senior English teacher at the school, that young Dylan was brilliant in English but inattentive in every other class. By the age of ten he had decided to become a poet. Answering some questions in 1951, Thomas recalled what first led him to "love language and want to work *in* it and *for* it": "nursery rhymes and folk tales, the Scottish Ballads, a few lines of hymns, the most famous Bible stories and the rhythms of the Bible, Blake's Songs of Innocence, and the quite incomprehensible magical majesty and nonsense of Shakespeare heard, read, and near-murdered in the

first forms of my school."[2] His reading immediately
patterned his apprentice efforts; and he imitated
(according to his own listing) Sir Thomas Browne,
de Quincey, Henry Newbolt, the Ballads, Blake,
Baroness Orczy, Marlowe, Chums, the Imagists, the
Bible, Poe, Keats, Lawrence, Anon., and Shakespeare.[3]
His friend Daniel Jones remembers Yeats, Richard
Aldington, Sacheverell Sitwell, D. H. Lawrence, and
Hopkins as active influences on Thomas' early development.[4] When Thomas arrived in London in
1934 and met Geoffrey Grigson, he publicly "pre-
ferred" Rosetti, Francis Thompson, James Thomson
(B.V.), and Stephen Spender.[5] At twenty-one he
reviewed with great aplomb the new two-volume
John Clare for the *Adelphi*.[6] In the three years after
the war Thomas did about a hundred broadcasts,
mainly readings of, and talks on, other writers. This
work culminated in the flawless public reading performances of a wide variety of poetry.[7]

T. S. Eliot (with his notes to *The Waste Land*)
and Yeats (with *A Vision*) have made clear how
much of their poetry was written within reach of
their books. Thomas has not; and this default tempts
us to picture him writing, for example, the *Ballad of
the Long-legged Bait* with Rimbaud's *Bateau ivre* in
one hand and Donne's *The Baite* in the other. Thomas,
however, has made a few facts clear: "I do wish I
had learned some other languages apart from English,
BBC Third Programme, and saloon. Then perhaps I
could understand what some people mean when they
say I have been influenced by Rimbaud."[8] And it
seems rather odd to think of Donne's short love poem
— or any poem, for that matter — as a source for

a *Ballad* whose composition took over a hundred arduously worked sheets of paper.[9] If Thomas was really depending on Rimbaud or Donne for any aspect of form or content, he certainly made a very convincing show of the opposite. Again, *On the Marriage of a Virgin* has been said to echo Marvell's *The Gallery* on the ground that a series of images, "dawn," "thighs," "dove," etc., have the same order of appearance in both poems.[10] However, for this poem too we have Thomas' draft, which shows no such given patterning. Finally, the suggestion that *We lying by seasand* has a source in Rilke's Second Duino Elegy[11] fails, if for no other reason, because the poem is dated 1933 and Thomas had not read much Rilke until 1941.[12]

The question of specific sources is worth taking up because the negative answer supports what we instinctively feel about Thomas' poems: that they are new and unique, that no one ever wrote poems like these before, and that readers of Thomas have to begin without preconceptions. How convenient it would be if what we learned in reading Hopkins, the favorite candidate for general influence on the poet, could really be applied to Thomas. But the similarity between Hopkins and Thomas is only superficial. When Hopkins writes "Miracle-in-Mary-of-flame" he has dislocated normal English usage for special effects of both alliteration and meaning. When Thomas writes "Christ-cross-row of death," Hopkensian though it may seem, our reaction must be geared to entirely new principles. There is no dislocation of syntax here, no deliberate straining for effects of sound. Anyone interested in the antiquity of Thomas' compound noun should refer to the Oxford English Dictionary; it is as old, and as simple, as ABC.[13]

Again, how convenient if the key to Thomas were in Welsh poetry. But Welsh poetry is more difficult to write than to read, and Thomas had no incentive to do either. Those who would like to have Thomas be a "bard" and yet acknowledge that he did not know or study Welsh see Hopkins as the germ-carrier.[14] But a poet cannot be smickled with Welsh by casual contact; the restrictive Welsh forms by their very nature require labored, self-conscious application. Hopkins wrote a couple of poems in Welsh and comes as close as anyone to utilizing *cynghanedd* in English; but if there are one or two lines in Thomas that fit the Welsh patterns it is purely accidental.[15] The particular hoops that Thomas set himself to jump through were quite different.

There must be hoops of a kind. A poet sometimes besets himself with the most excessive obstacles to producing a poem, instinctively knowing that the energy generated in overcoming them vitalizes the final result. Count the number of syllables per line in the seven stanzas of *Poem in October* and one set of Thomas' hoops becomes apparent:

1.	9	12	9	3	5	12	12	5	3	9
2.	9	12	9	3	5	12	12	5	3	9
3.	9	12	9	3	5	12	12	5	3	9
4.	9	12	9	3	5	12	12	5	3	9
5.	9	12	9	3	5	12	12	5	3	9
6.	9	12	9	3	5	<u>13</u>	12	5	3	9
7.	9	12	9	3	5	<u>12</u>	12	5	3	9

If this regularity should strike anyone as fortuitous,

he may refer to Daniel Jones on Thomas' concern for syllable counting[16] and to the poet's work sheets for *Over Sir John's hill*, where syllable totals are put against the lines in a few of the trials with, in one place, an urgent note to his muse: "3 more syllables."[17] Actually, as Thomas approached the end of his work on *Over Sir John's hill* and felt the rightness of certain lines that unfortunately had the wrong number of syllables, it was the syllabic pattern that suffered. The final poem is not absolutely regular, but one would hardly call it unfinished.[18] The inexplicable thirteen syllable line in the sixth stanza of *Poem in October* is another case in point. The self-imposed discipline is strange, the truancy from it stranger; yet both are understandable. A poet has to lever himself into action, knowing the terribly hard work it is to fill a page with original and important utterance. Thomas put the problem well, with customary understatement:

> Sometimes it feels very good to have a blank piece of paper in front of you, and you put down the first line. Then you look at all the paper and think, Now I've got to rhyme this. And it's work. Oh God, it's awful![19]

The intricate syllable and rhyme schemes are tricks the poet uses on himself in order to get the next line written.

But the situation is not adequately described as donkey following carrot, for Thomas was a beast of burden with somewhere to go each time he set out. The carrot, the incidental reward in meeting strict verse forms, is only used in the face of a momentary paralysis at having too much to say, of knowing full well what agony the journey to the final poem involves. The main hurdle Thomas puts before himself is his devotion to a personal and perhaps fleeting truth and to finding the image that can express the truth so that it stays true for the duration of the poem. Thomas' truths are such that it is sheer flippancy to list them as birth, copulation, and death. It is best to approach them as closely as we can in the poems themselves, where we as readers can, as much as possible, find them true.

In any case, Thomas' bookshelves, along with the other icons in the photograph, have to be placed well into the background. Thomas obviously had access to a good dictionary from an early age (or perhaps words like *parhelion* and *hyleg* were commonplace in Swansea Grammar School in 1931?). But his reading was probably very haphazard, done — if according to his own prescription — while hanging by his ears from the chandeliers.[20] Though the reading is not to be slighted on that account, it is of little use in illuminating any particular poem. With Thomas there is no prerequisite reading list. Thomas' obscurity is not aristocratic; it can be tackled with general knowledge and a good dictionary, tools democratic enough.

[2]

Since his poems have this kind of availability, it is surprising that Thomas' reputation should rest on so few poems that are well understood. His *Collected*

Poems moves rather like an iceberg; nine-tenths of its power and weight is under the surface, sensed by us but not clearly visible. In this situation our main concern will be the precise nature of Thomas' obscurity — or, to put it a better way, the precise nature of our difficulty with Thomas' poetic idiom, for Thomas will undoubtedly become easier to read and understand as time goes on.

Most poets are aware of the pitfalls of their particular mode of communication, the danger of purely personal imagery; and they recognize that in the final analysis the words must be objectively meaningful. They may postulate for themselves a most persistent and ingenious reader, but they know they must treat him right. They cannot pretend that he will follow their secret thoughts. They must in the long run make their intention plain in one way or another. Granted that Dylan Thomas writes about common things in a most uncommon way, he always (or almost always) gives the necessary clues to the reader. The extraordinary is subject to ordinary interpretation.

Let us take a look at one of his favorite techniques. Thomas' instinct to create an original vision from the everyday event leads him to use clichés and common phrases, just altered to the extent that we have to think them out afresh, but within the aura of their familiarity. He brings to the front of the mind what was always at the back of it. One main source of difficulty in Thomas is the ingenuity of this kind of dislocation. For instance, in the following passage, the opening of *A Child's Christmas in Wales*, Thomas plays very innocently, as befits a children's story, on the common phrases "around the corner" and "out of sound." The epithet "two-tongued sea" later in the paragraph is deceptively simple, however, and worth looking into:

> One Christmas was so much like another, in those years around the sea-town corner now and out of all sound except the distant speaking voices I sometimes hear a moment before sleep, that I can never remember whether it snowed for six days and six nights when I was twelve or whether it snowed for twelve days and twelve nights when I was six. All the Christmases roll down toward the two-tongued sea, like a cold and head-long moon bundling down the sky that was our street; and they stop at the rim of the ice-edged, fish-freezing waves, and I plunge my hands in the snow and bring out what-ever I can find. In goes my hand into that wool-white bell - tongued ball of holidays resting at the rim of the carol-singing sea, and out comes Mrs. Prothero and the fire-men.[21]

End of paragraph. What the poet is saying is familiar enough: he dips into his rather jumbled memories of Christmases he has known as a child, and one partic-ular incident occurs to him. But, even in this prose piece, Thomas' strange imagination is at work, and he pictures his memories as a cumulative snowball rolling to the edge of the sea of oblivion. His act of recalling the past is like putting his hand (literally dipping) into that snowball, "that wool-white bell-tongued ball of holidays." "Wool-white" is easy. The ball is "bell-tongued" and "of holidays" because the memories are all associated with holidays from school and Christmas bells. Bells, of course, have tongues, literally, and metaphorically since they call out to us. Seas, however, have tongues only in imagination, and there is certainly no imaginable reason for the sea's mouth to have more than one tongue in order to receive the rolling snowball. Yet there is an easefulness about the phrase "two-tongued"; and if one substitutes "two-faced" one recognizes the familiar ring. The "distant speaking voices" heard just before sleep come out of the sea of forgetfulness *defectively* — it's as though the sea were deceiving him. He can't recall whether it snowed six days and nights when he was twelve or twelve days and nights when he was six. The confusing voices give him two versions; the sea has thus two tongues. "Two-tongued," we conclude, is simply a summary phrase for his humorously defective memory. The logic of the image is both naive and circuitous, extraordinary in effect but of quite ordinary ingredients. Image is connected to image by perverse logic, uninhibited leaps of childlike cunning involving word-plays. For instance, when the sea is mentioned again toward the end of the paragraph, it is the "carol-singing" sea. Having tongues, it can obviously sing. But the idea of deceit has been dropped; there is no deep connection between the two ways of describing the sea. In the poetry, images are often connected in an equally spurious and fanciful manner, but a deeper connection is found in the underlying, serious themes shared by the several disparate images.

We have tried to be precise about Thomas' "two-tongued sea." Can the image be pinned down in this way? Isn't there room for doubt? Of course, there always is room; but reasonable certainty is a legitimate goal. Obscurity does not necessarily imply ambiguity. Unless Thomas was as two-faced as his sea, he had some definite idea in mind when he wrote the image, and was not interested in giving scope for loose guesswork. Consider a possible alternative: a serpent traditionally has two tongues and is a symbol of deceit. The objections to seeing the serpent in the image are, first, the general rule in explication (as in scientific common sense) that the simpler explanation for any phenomenon, other things being equal, must be correct; and, second, the equally basic rule that nothing can be said to exist unless its presence makes a difference to the environment. Had Thomas really meant us to see this intermediary symbolic presence he would have been bound to use the serpent again in context. He doesn't do so. Thus there is no reason to see the serpent there at all. A word or phrase may have two or more meanings, but only those definite meanings that work successfully in context.

Such principles are more easily stated than applied. The two-tongued sea-serpent doesn't work; but there is a more nagging possibility to consider. In the earlier version, "Memories of Christmas" (1945), the sentence in question read:

> All the Christmases roll down the hill toward the Welsh-speaking sea. . . .

"Welsh-speaking" is an incidental adjective, informing us that the setting is Wales. One should note that, in this early version, the sentence is in a new paragraph, a dozen lines away from "the speaking of the voices." Revision (for *Harper's Bazaar* 1950) cut out the intervening lines, and the adjective "Welsh - speaking" must have become unbearably gratuitous (it was gratuitous in the first place). Thomas had used "the bilingual sea" in "Quite Early One Morning" (1945), so that "two-tongued" was a product of a natural piece of wordplay.

With this Anglo-Welsh sea around, were we too hasty in seeing "two-tongued" as describing the two messages of the sea voices? The answer, I think, must be no. The slightly self-mocking notion of defective memory is well summed up in "two-tongued." Our first interpretation is very effective — the "bilingual" interpretation less so. We should not deny Thomas credit for the best legitimate meaning we can find. Is the idea of "Welsh-speaking" retained in the image at all now? The answer here is difficult. One might wish to say no; but, once thought of (and, quite possibly, thought of without the textual variants), this meaning is impossible to shake off altogether. I rather think that the words "two-tongued" recommended themselves to Thomas because in the new and worthier conceit he could still be reminded of his former thought.

This sort of poetic licence suits some readers better than others. One has good reason to be wary; unlimited "extra" meanings become available as targets once licence is given to shoot at random. I am sure it was not the poet's intention to give such licence. In each case we should try our best to obey the poet's precise intention.[22] The idea of a "Welsh-speaking" sea is not *necessary* in the final phrasing of the passage above; it is *permissible*, I think, as an extra meaning subsidiary to the meaning that does the main work in context. The validity of secondary meanings is the stickiest of all questions in Dylan Thomas studies. In the final analysis, whether or not a meaning works successfully in context is a matter of opinion; but one trusts that common sense *is* common, and that agreement on such points can generally be reached.

Again, this implies that Thomas has as much regard for common sense as his readers. A plea for trust in Thomas' good faith and ultimate intelligibility is not unwarranted. Anyone who has heard the poet's recordings will know the insistence and reassurance in his voice, perhaps his most compelling weapon against oblivion. But, turning from the recordings to the printed page, the reader might have his confidence in the poet severely shaken when he tries the opening lines of the *Collected Poems*:

> I see the boys of summer in their ruin
> Lay the gold tithings barren,
> Setting no store by harvest, freeze the soils;
> There in their heat the winter floods
> Of frozen loves they fetch their girls,
> And drown the cargoed apples in their tides.

This, and much more of Thomas, is so uncompromising that the recordings take on great importance. Thomas' vitality and seriousness in those performances are his pledge with the reader. After *hearing* Thomas we are much less likely to assume that such lines as the above are merely self-willed and chaotic.

Faith in Thomas' meaningfulness is not, of course, a prerequisite, merely a useful way to begin. The proof of the poetry's coherence is in the finding of it. The greater part of this book is the seeking of that proof. The first lines of Thomas' first volume have been raised as a challenge; one cannot do better than begin there:

I see the boys of summer in their ruin.

Who are the "boys of summer"? If there were a specific answer, if they were fisher princes in the Grail legend or a Swansea boys' club, say, we would have no need to hesitate.[23] But the boys are apparently Thomas' original conception. Their significance is both universal and important; we do not realize the extent of it until we have absorbed all that they do in the poem, which is a great deal by the end. In this first stanza alone, their actions have such variety and range that they are bewildering at first. They "lay gold tithings barren." "Tithings" are sheaves of wheat, ripe and golden. The boys are ruining the harvest, setting no store by it, actively countering it by freezing the soils. The boys bring cold love to their girls; they negate warm affection and prevent the harvest of sexual fulfilment. They drown ripe apples — another expression of the ruin of harvest.

As before with the "two-tongued sea" (i.e. a sea with two tongues), we begin by taking the words as literally as possible. "Gold tithings," for instance, is not merely a code phrase for something else. Wheat sheaves are to be seen as laid down and left barren. Thomas often demands that we take as perceivable what is usually considered non-material. An abstraction such as "loves" becomes part of a winter flood. The "winter floods of frozen loves" is a way of describing affection at its coldest; but it is the nature of Thomas' metaphor that the two strands be distinctly intertwined: the glimpse of ice floes and the notion of coldness in love. Further, in reiterating the phrase "ruin of harvest" in the above discussion, we are discovering a common ground for all these actions; each can be seen as symbolizing in its own way the same single concept. In the end, some abstract term such as "nullification" or "the negative principle" is necessary to summarize the significance of the boys so that no part of their behavior contradicts or stands outside the summary. But even this will not suffice; as we go into parts II and III of the poem we begin to realize that the boys are constructive in their destructiveness. We need a concept that incorporates both growth and decay, because the boys cause both. Biology provides a convenient term in *metabolism*, with its constituent processes, anabolism (building up of cells) and catabolism (breaking down of cells). Thomas is very conscious of the precarious balance that nature sustains every day in the human body and in the cosmos. A notable expression of this balance comes at the end of *Fern Hill*: "Time held me green and dying." In his green growing youth the poet felt the pull of death. The boys of summer personify these two forces; they too are green (part II, l. 14), but in their ruin. *I see the boys of summer* is an all-embracing poem. Thomas chose it to head his first book, *18 Poems;* it retains its pride of place in the *Collected Poems*. The chronology of composition shows that, far from being the earliest of the *18 Poems*, it was written at the height of the poetic fervor that produced the volume. It is, perhaps, first in importance. We shall use it to take the brunt of analysis in Chapter II.

Chapter II

Explications and Explanations

"Contraries are positives"

William Blake, title page
of *Milton*, Book the Second

I SEE THE BOYS OF SUMMER

I

I see the boys of summer in their ruin
Lay the gold tithings barren,
Setting no store by harvest, freeze the soils;
There in their heat the winter floods
Of frozen loves they fetch their girls,
And drown the cargoed apples in their tides.

These boys of light are curdlers in their folly,
Sour the boiling honey;
The jacks of frost they finger in the hives;
There in the sun the frigid threads
Of doubt and dark they feed their nerves;
The signal moon is zero in their voids.

I see the summer children in their mothers
Split up the brawned womb's weathers,
Divide the night and day with fairy thumbs;
There in the deep with quartered shades
Of sun and moon they paint their dams
As sunlight paints the shelling of their heads.

I see that from these boys shall men of nothing
Stature by seedy shifting,
Or lame the air with leaping from its heats;
There from their hearts the dogdayed pulse
Of love and light bursts in their throats.
O see the pulse of summer in the ice.

II

But seasons must be challenged or they totter
Into a chiming quarter
Where, punctual as death, we ring the stars;
There, in his night, the black-tongued bells
The sleepy man of winter pulls,
Nor blows back moon-and-midnight as she
blows.

We are the dark deniers, let us summon
Death from a summer woman,
A muscling life from lovers in their cramp,
From the fair dead who flush the sea
The bright-eyed worm on Davy's lamp,
And from the planted womb the man of straw.

We summer boys in this four-winded spinning,
Green of the seaweeds' iron,
Hold up the noisy sea and drop her birds,
Pick the world's ball of wave and froth
To choke the deserts with her tides,
And comb the county gardens for a wreath.

In spring we cross our foreheads with the holly,
Heigh ho the blood and berry,
And nail the merry squires to the trees;   ) Christmas &
Here love's damp muscle dries and dies,   ) Easter; birth is
Here break a kiss in no love's quarry.   death
O see the poles of promise in the boys.

III

I see you boys of summer in your ruin.
Man in his maggot's barren.
And boys are full and foreign in the pouch.
I am the man your father was.
We are the sons of flint and pitch.
O see the poles are kissing as they cross.

Any attempt to justify the ways of God to man,
even one by so young a poet as Thomas at the time
this poem was written, is interesting. What Milton
wanted to justify, and what Thomas here faces, is,
in its simplest terms, the existence of death. Thomas
does not draw on theology. His frame of reference
is not the after-life but the present cosmos; and he
values death because it makes possible the miraculous
renewal of life. We suggested in the last chapter that
the boys of summer personify the basic forces of
growth and decay seen by Thomas operating every-
where in the universe. We used the term metabolism,
a concept that would have been congenial to Thomas.
Biology shows that the breaking down process is
essential to growth. It is this interdependence between
life and death forces that Thomas is portraying in
I see the boys of summer.

In the Mutability Cantos of the *Faerie Queene*
Spenser allows the Goddess Mutability to have her
full say before he finally asserts her ravages to be
part of a higher order of nature. Thomas follows a
similar plan, for only in part II of the poem is the
positive role of the boys of summer brought out. In
part I they act like enthusiastic agents of Mutability,
showing

How MUTABILITY in them doth play
Her cruell sports, to many mens decay
                              (VII.vi.1).

"Cruel sports" describes well the actions of the boys
in these first stanzas. They have an air of gaiety about
them in the midst of utmost cruelty. Their paradox-
ical nature is in the first line: they are "of summer"
and "in ruin" at the same time. One might picture
bare-foot, ill-clad urchins; but "summer" and "ruin"
are only casually effective as description. They are
symbolic: "summer" sums up a series of qualities
associated with the season of warmth and well-being,
growth and harvest-time; "ruin" finds an echo in all
the destructive acts against the qualities of summer.
Once the larger themes are established—as here by
the two key words "summer" and "ruin" in the first
line—the symbolic images of the rest of the poem
fall into place. The boys take "gold tithings" (*summer*) and "lay them barren" (*ruin*). They "set no
store" (*ruin*) "by harvest" (*summer*). They "freeze"
(*ruin*) the "soils" (*summer*). "In their heat" (*summer*) they "fetch their girls" (*summer*) "the winter
floods of frozen loves" (*ruin*). They "drown in their
tides" (*ruin*) "cargoed apples" (*summer*). Since *summer* is positive (+) and *ruin* negative (−), the second
stanza can be put:

> These boys of light (+) are curdlers in their
>   folly (−),
> Sour (−) the boiling honey (+);
> The jacks of frost (−) they finger in the
>   hives (+);
> There in the sun (+) the frigid threads
> Of doubt and dark (−) they feed their nerves;

The signal moon (+) is zero in their voids (−).

An expectation is set up, and we sometimes grasp the significance of an action before the details of it. This short cut to the symbolic level (along with the hypnotic rhythms) makes it possible to enjoy Thomas' poetry without understanding very much of it. But Thomas meant the poems to be understood on the immediate literal level. He used the word "literal" on one occasion as a way of insisting that the *details* of his images be attended to:

> Miss Edith Sitwell's analysis, in a letter to the *Sunday Times* of the lines:
>
>> The atlas-eater with a jaw for news
>> Bit out the mandrake with to-mor-
>>   row's scream
>
>> *Altarwise by owl-light*
>
> seems to me very vague. She says the lines refer to "the violent speed and the sensation-loving, horror-loving craze of modern life." She doesn't take the literal meaning: that a world-devouring ghost creature bit out the horror of to-morrow from a gentleman's loins.[1]

No matter what the full meaning of *Altarwise by owl-light* may be, Thomas evidently wants us to see his "atlas-eater" as something which actually devours worlds and is specifically biting off a mandrake in the quoted lines. He drives the point home by going on to say: "This poem is a particular incident in a particular adventure, not a general elliptical deprecation of this 'horrible, crazy, speed-life.'" We trust that he is not denying the particular adventure all general significance, but just stressing that one must work from the literal level.

The trouble with the literal interpretation of some of Thomas' lines is not in seeing what happens but in believing it. Thomas has the boys drown cargoed apples in their tides. The boys have, in some unspecified sense, tides, in which they drown apples that are, in some unspecified sense, cargoed. One can imagine apples sinking in the sea; but can one *believe* that this is what Thomas wants us to imagine? There is actually good reason to do so. Thomas once wrote to Vernon Watkins concerning two lines from *I make this in a warring absence*, "A calm wind blows that raised the trees like hair / Once where the soft snow's blood was turned to ice":

> a wind had blown that had frightened everything and created the first ice and the first frost by frightening the falling snow so much that the blood of each flake froze.[2]

Again the lines are a particular incident in a particular adventure. They utilize the two common expressions for fear: "his hair stood on end" (the trees' hair, the branches) and "his blood froze" (here, the blood of each snowflake). The thought can be reduced to one word, "fear"; but Thomas requires us to see the literal event in the metaphor for fear: "the blood of each flake froze."[3] So that he would also, one can be sure, want us to see the apples drown in the tides — then we are free to see the event as another symbol of the ruin of harvest.

Of course, if we are asked to accept that **cargoed**

apples are drowned, we should also be assured that
cargoed pears or plums wouldn't have done just as
well. This assurance usually comes with an understanding of the metaphor involved; the words earn
their place by a sort of second, hidden meaning
(which is what "metaphor" implies). With the image
of the snow's blood freezing, the middle stage was
the common expression for fear. With the cargoed
apples, no such midway point comes immediately to
mind. "Cargoed" is an interesting word: the apples
are ripe, heavy, cargoed with their own weight; and
since cargoed, they are like ships that can sink. If
there must be some thing for which the phrase is a
metaphor, I suggest the apples are the breasts of the
girls in the previous line. Compare "jacks of frost"
in the second stanza:

> These boys of light are curdlers in their folly,
> Sour the boiling honey;
> The jacks of frost they finger in the hives.

"Jacks of frost" is a metaphor for icicles. The poet
is playing on the name Jack Frost and also giving
the image a sexual twist, the slang meaning of "jack,"
common enough in England, providing the male
counterpart to the hollow hive of the female. The
boys again bring "frozen loves" to their girls. If we
also think of "jack of hearts" with its connotations
of knavery, we have quite a complicated superstruc-
ture for the phrase. It is Thomas' practice to take
some common item such as an icicle and describe it
with deliberate strangeness to bring out certain constituent qualities. Thus in part II of *I see the boys of
summer* the phrase "this four-winded spinning" de-

scribes the revolving globe of this planet in terms of appropriate qualities, its four-windedness and its spinning. Here the icicle image fits the boys of summer: it is a stiff, prodding weapon of destructive mischief, cold and male in its attack on female warmth.

Thomas sanctioned the search for double meanings in his poetry when he said that a line from *A grief ago*:

> The country-handed grave boxed into love

meant that "the grave had a country for each hand, that it raised those hands up and boxed the hero of my poem into love. 'Boxed' has the coffin and the pug-glove in it."[4] The grave is heavy-handed, so Thomas' image acts out the inherent event in the metaphor, giving the grave a country for each hand, hands heavy enough. The coffin, itself a box, is an unavoidable threat, a violent coercer like a heavy-handed boxer. In the same way as he would have said of "jacks of frost" that "it has male stiffness and icicles in it," so Thomas is unequivocally saying that "boxed" contains both the coffin and the pug-glove. This process of adding secondary and tertiary connotations to an image is a risky business. In the third stanza of *I see the boys of summer*, "fairy thumbs" comes with something of a jolt:

> I see the summer children in their mothers
> Split up the brawned womb's weathers,
> Divide the night and day with fairy thumbs.

Just for the sake of argument, are we to accept the connotations of homosexuality in this word? Or, if we refuse to do so, on what basis do we refuse?

Thomas can be ruthlessly double-edged if he wants
to. Take a most poignant line from the later poem
In the white giant's thigh. Dead women buried in the
dust of the hillside pull the poet down to them:

> Now [the women] clasp me to their grains
>   in the gigantic glade.

"Grains" is dust, but it is also "groins." The embrace
becomes sexual. Besides the verbal echo of "groins"
in the word, "grains" actually means "groin" in a
dialect meaning that Thomas could have known.[5] But,
of all the possible verbal puns hovering around the
word "grains" ("groans," "greens," "grins," and so
on), we accept "groins" chiefly because it is pertinent
to the major theme of the poem — the sexual longing
of the childless women — while the alternatives make
no such direct connection with the themes that were
Thomas' preoccupation. "Fairy" is perhaps sufficiently
explained by the delicate, diminutive thumbs that
children in the womb might be imagined to have,
and their magical, fairy-like dividing of night and
day. If one were to press for a double meaning to
help the word earn its place, the word "changelings"
(a species of fairy) might come to mind: these are
certainly children of mutability and change — and,
possibly, in Thomas' logic, changelings.

   We cannot, however, dodge the fact that
Thomas knew exactly what he was risking with that
word. In an unpublished letter to Trevor Hughes
three months before the poem, he used the phrase
"like a fairy" and felt compelled to go on: "It needed
courage to say that 'like a fairy', for the young panto-
mime ladies, gallivanting in gossamer nudity, have

robbed the fairy of all but her woman's body. A fairy
is not supernatural; she is the most natural thing in
the world." Thomas in the New Year 1934 was
"believing in" fairies. There is the literal fairy in
"fairy thumbs," then. What about the slang "fairy"?
He had used the word in conjunction with "epicene"
in a Notebook poem 18 of March 1931. Yet the "fairy
thumbs" in our poem is not revolting, as homosexuality was to Thomas ("It's the only vice, I think, that
revolts me," he wrote in another unpublished letter
about this time). The word "hermaphrodite" — used
without disparagement in another early poem — gives
us a better clue. If "fairy" is thought to contain both
male and female, it is certainly polar; and the in-
determinacy of sex is appropriate to the foetus image.

With this third stanza of *I see the boys of summer* we have a new locale, the womb of the mother;
and we might wish to question the logic which has
brought us from the harvest field of the first stanza
to the womb of the third. The "particular adventure"
has a strange sequence of events. Is there any narrative at all, in the ordinary sense of the word? Thomas
tried to express his idea of narrative in an answer to
an enquiry from *New Verse:*

> Narrative, in its widest sense, satisfies what
> Eliot, talking of "meaning," calls "one habit
> of the reader." Let the narrative take that
> one logical habit of the reader along with its
> movement, and the essence of the poem will
> do its work on him.[6]

A reader habitually expects *something* to happen to
someone in a poem; Thomas intends to meet this

expectation. His poems are filled with action; and the reader does find himself swept along the narrative line by force of habit, even though the different events are not in an accustomed sequence of cause and effect, of temporal and spacial contiguity. It seems like a surrealist world where actions follow one another without reason. But is it really surrealistic? Behind the many actions of the boys of summer we found the abstract concept of negation. The disparate actions have unity on that level. They are connected (as Webster's *NID* defines *disparate*) "by some notion of great generality or by some interest of extreme catholicity." Furthermore, the way in which the imaged actions succeed each other is not entirely haphazard. Disparateness is the essence of Thomas' style:

> A poem by myself *needs* a host of images, because its centre is a host of images. I make one image—though "make" is not the word; I let, perhaps, an image be "made" emotionally in me and then apply to it what intellectual and critical forces I possess — let it breed another, let that image contradict the first, make, of the third image bred out of the other two together, a fourth contradictory image, and let them all, within my imposed formal limits, conflict. Each image holds within it the seed of its own destruction, and my dialectal method, as I understand it, is a constant building up and breaking down of the images that come out of the central seed, which is itself destructive and constructive at the same time.[7]

A poet's rationalization of his own creative act may offer all kinds of traps; but here Thomas seems to give genuine help in understanding how to follow the "logic" of his images. Let us take our stanza two:

> These boys of light are curdlers in their folly,
> Sour the boiling honey;
> The jacks of frost they finger in the hives;
> There in the sun the frigid threads
> Of doubt and dark they feed their nerves;
> The signal moon is zero in their voids.

"Curdlers" of the first line breeds the "sour" of the second, utilizing the alternative meaning of sour: milk *curdles* but honey is made *unsweet*. The posing of citric sourness against lactic sourness is not astounding — but Thomas said nothing about violent contradictions. It is enough to see that the first image prompts the second, which is, however, not really a continuation of it but something new. Similarly, the "boiling honey" gives rise to "hives," which again involves a new image of negation: fingering and freezing. The boys then feed into their nerves the frigid threads (bred from "jacks of frost") of doubt and dark: a different image from the preceding and again "contradictory" in the sense that it thwarts our expectation of a continuing locale.

This breeding and contradicting process is essentially fanciful and undisciplined; its only logic is that of association of ideas. "Sun" in line 4 of the stanza above suggests "moon" for line 6; "nerves" in line 5 makes the moon a "signal" moon; and having fed on doubt and dark in line 5, the boys are possessed of "voids" in line 6. The signal moon, in keeping with the harvest theme of the first stanza, is the full moon (a sign of changing weather); the boys make its roundness a mere zero, an emptiness, so it ceases to be a signal. This is an effective image. Being cosmic in scope, it is the climactic incident in this series of "adventures." But, for most of us, this virtue is obscured by the disjointedness of the narrative. Thomas wants us to go with him along a literal narrative line; but in these early poems he does not give us the habitual narrative signposts, and it is something of an effort to hold on. This does not detract from the effectiveness of the images as symbolic of the central concept of the poem. The moon, traditionally a harvest and female fertility symbol, is made zero by the boys — this is very effective in communicating their destructiveness symbolically. Nor should our present difficulty with the narrative of disparate images prevent us from seeing that it is the very disparateness which ensures the broadness of the symbolized concept. The "jacks of frost" could be taken entirely on a sexual plane; but add the "signal moon" and the interpretation must be pushed further back into a more generalized notion beyond sex. Add the further images, and the final result is a concept of life and death which is as broad as it is because each image has helped to define its breadth. And this is where the discipline comes in. Each image must be shaped to perform this function of creating the final concept as well as carrying on a narrative line. No matter how casually the images are bred, they must meet the demands of this symbolic function. Thomas said:

> Out of the inevitable conflict of images —
> inevitable, because of the creative, recreative,
> destructive and contradictory nature of the
> motivating centre, the womb of war — I try
> to make that momentary peace which is a
> poem.[8]

The reconciliation is in the unifying concept shared by all the images. We have a grip on the meaning of a poem when we understand on what basic premise the warring images are reconciled.

The womb symbolism of stanza three is self-evidently consistent with the life-cycle theme of *I see the boys of summer* as a whole:

> I see the summer children in their mothers
> Split up the brawned womb's weathers,
> Divide the night and day with fairy thumbs;
> There in the deep with quartered shades
> Of sun and moon they paint their dams
> As sunlight paints the shelling of their heads.

"Signal moon" of the previous stanza brought up the subject of weather; here the womb has "weathers." Weathers are the conditions through which time and the seasons work their changes on the world. By transposition they become the atmospheric conditions within the human body, specifically here within the "brawned," muscular womb. What does it mean to "split up" these weathers? Since the children here are presumably the unborn boys of summer, they will be up to their usual tricks as agents of mutability. Nowhere are time and change more dramatically portrayed than in gestation, in which splitting up and reduplication of cells occurs. Pregnancy makes us very conscious of the calendar, makes its demands continuously night and day. This vital sense of change through time is utilized by the poet here. Not that "splitting up weathers" need refer to any particular stage of pregnancy; Thomas is not interested in taking us into a real human drama. On one level, the thought is very literal: the summer children take the weathers of the womb (the conditions in the womb) and split them up (an action of producing multiple from single). It is as though the first day of Genesis were repeated by each child within its mother, peace and unity destroyed by the presence of another being, the fight of opposites begun. One becomes two, two becomes four: this is the development within the stanza. The shades of color with which the children paint their mother are "quartered," an indication of increasing multiplicity (as in such birth poems as *From love's first fever to her plague:* "And the four winds, that had long blown as one"). "Quartered" is a pun-word, since both the year and the month have quarters, which are sometimes symbolized on the calendar by a small circle shaded in quadrants. The children are painting the seasons on their mothers. "Dams" is some indication of the harshness of the act. The birth of a child has often been seen by poets as the beginning of the death of the parents. As the child grows through nine months in the amniotic deep of the womb, its first gift to the parent is a sense of mortality. As the sun, the creative force, paints the shelling of its head (creates the skull, the pieced-together shell which gets a coloring of hair), the child paints ("tarnishes" as it were) the mother with the touch of age.

After his glance back at the boys of summer as an emblem of Time in the womb, the poet looks ahead, in the fourth stanza, to the boys' growing up. They will become "men of nothing," hollow men:

> I see that from these boys shall men of nothing
> Stature by seedy shifting,
> Or lame the air with leaping from its heats;
> There from their hearts the dogdayed pulse
> Of love and light bursts in their throats.
> O see the pulse of summer in the ice.

"Seedy shifting," a reminder that in a sense the gestation of the womb continues in the metabolism of the body, has unhealthy connotations in the words "seedy" and "shifting" (reminding one of "shifty"). After negating the harvest and their mothers, the boys now negate themselves. It is a vision of their ruin; they will leap away from their own heat of summer, crippling the air (a violent enough leap) and presumably themselves. Just as "lame" is apparently bred from "stature" and "leaping" from "shifting," so "dogdayed" comes from the "heats." Again there is a contradiction: the heat (dogdays are in July and August) now "bursts in their throats" — throbs, pulsates, in their throats. It is surprising that the boys should have so much "love and light" in their hearts. It would be more surprising if the image were less violent.[9] The reversal is from one extreme to another. The boys have all along been "of summer," but belying their summeriness with ice and cold. In these last three lines we begin to see the "pulse of summer in the ice." And even their heat is excessive. They are symbolic of polar opposites of whatever kind. As agents of change, they contain all weathers, and are capable of pulling each season slowly or violently into its opposite.

[2]

The "But" which starts off part II of *I see the boys of summer* suggests its opposition to the tone of accusation of part I. Here the boys speak for themselves and defend mutability:

> But seasons must be challenged or they totter
> Into a chiming quarter
> Where, punctual as death, we ring the stars;
> There, in his night, the black-tongued bells
> The sleepy man of winter pulls,
> Nor blows back moon-and-midnight as she
>   blows.

The first line is as close as we get to a direct statement of theme: seasons (standing for all the different states in the world and in life) must be fought against or they will stagnate. The "chiming quarter" (echoing "quartered shades," a previous symbol of mortality) is a place where clock-like monotony reigns. One has to ring star after star as though each were a bell-chime that had to be sounded punctually. Death is punctual and is ever present in the ticking of a clock. The sleepy man of winter is a deliberate opposite of the boys of summer. Representing stagnation, he pulls the bell ropes of death, the bell tongues in mourning black. He exists in the very dead of night ("moon-and-midnight") and he does not resist the

dark, fails to answer the call in the night. There is
no pulse of summer in his ice.

The boys, however, do blow back. They are
great gainsayers:

> We are the dark deniers, let us summon
> Death from a summer woman,
> A muscling life from lovers in their cramp,
> From the fair dead who flush the sea
> The bright-eyed worm on Davy's lamp,
> And from the planted womb the man of straw.

"Deniers" is a key word. All the subsequent actions
are denials — in a sense that we gradually become
fully aware of: to deny is not only to pull down the
positive good (though this was the emphasis of part I)
but also to oppose the negative and produce good
from it. To produce death from a woman in the
summer of her life is obviously destructive denial;
but the next image is the reverse. "Muscling life"
(incidental echo of "brawned womb" here) is sum-
moned from the opposite, "cramp," lack of muscles.
("Cramp," however, is a paradox word, since it is
very expressive of the involuntary "death" in which
lovers beget life.) "Davy's lamp," which has superficial associations with the drowned through Davy
Jones, is the miner's lamp invented by Sir Humphrey
Davy; and the bright-eyed worm is its flame, like a
glowworm. Thomas uses "glow-worm" elsewhere as
a paradox word: a worm, usually associated with the
earth and death, is in this case a sparkling light. It is
a geological fact that oil comes from the long-decayed
organic deposits in the earth; like the glowworm, the
flame too is connected with the dead, the "fair"

dead, to complete the paradox. The dead produce the living flame. Another effective image of negative coming out of positive is "the man of straw" coming from "the planted womb," the womb planted with seed.

In the next stanza the boys continue their dual role:

> We summer boys in this four-winded spinning,
> Green of the seaweeds' iron,
> Hold up the noisy sea and drop her birds,
> Pick the world's ball of wave and froth
> To choke the deserts with her tides,
> And comb the county gardens for a wreath.

The boys are "green," virile, fresh — but green like seaweed, because of the iron content. Their greenness has a hard, metallic, ruthless quality inherent in it, and the world they live in, this four-winded spinning, is violent and inhumane. They hold up the noisy sea — one imagines a wave at its height arrested by these cosmic deniers — and drop the seabirds, presumably to destruction. They force the sea on to the deserts, choking them rather than parching their thirst. They search the county gardens not for the bouquet that the polite "county" might suggest, but for a stern wreath. Their greenness ends in a wreath, and then in the sharp holly:

> In spring we cross our foreheads with the holly,
> Heigh ho the blood and berry,
> And nail the merry squires to the trees;
> Here love's damp muscle dries and dies,
> Here break a kiss in no love's quarry.
> O see the poles of promise in the boys.

This stanza seems at first reading almost totally negative. Yet, it would be very strange for the poet to ask us to see "poles of promise" in the boys if such poles, positive as well as negative, had not been shown us. The positive is there, submerged in the apparently negative. For instance, within the anti-pastoral scene of the first three lines, there is a Christian symbolism that implies the opposite of destruction. The boys scratch a cross on their foreheads with holly (this itself reminds one of Christ's thorns), an act of cruelty and self-abnegation in the midst of gaiety. (The Elizabethan "Heigh ho" is both happy and sad; the berry is happy, the blood sad.) But the sign of the cross is also a blessing. Again, the nailing of the merry squires to the trees is not only an inhumanly perverse act but also a reminder of Easter, the crucifixion of Christ miraculously turned to good with the Redemption. The fortunate fall should indeed be merry. As an image for "poles of promise," is there anything more incisive than Christ on the Cross, depth of degradation signifying highest regeneration?

The two lines in which we might expect to see most clearly the "poles of promise" are

> Here love's damp muscle dries and dies,
> Here break a kiss in no love's quarry.

The first line is decidedly negative: "damp" is one of Thomas' ways of saying "life-containing," and dryness is death. Whatever part of the anatomy "love's damp muscle" might be, the line signifies the end of love. Does the breaking of the kiss in the next line mean the opposite, the beginning of love? Despite the negative sound of "break," there is rea-

son to think that it does. "Break" would normally
indicate that the kiss is destroyed, but think for a
moment of the logic of the image: breaking a kiss
in a quarry is basically a stone-breaking image. Here
we have the very making of the kiss, like a hammer
blow on a stone, a violent juncture. "Break" has the
same kind of positive implication that "bursts" had
in part I when it meant "pulsates." It is Thomas'
practice to use words of violence in order to speak
in hyperbolic terms of something essentially favored.
To "break a kiss in no love's quarry," then, is to
create love where there was none before, in the
quarry (suitably female) of no love. What more
direct opposite for "love's damp muscle" could be
found than the simple "no love's quarry"? The line
supplies the balancing positive pole, and we do, therefore, see the poles of life and death in the boys.

[3]

The single stanza of the third and last section of
I see the boys of summer suggests that it has four
times its apparent weight if it is to match the other
sections. It is a concentrated recapitulation and climax.

> I see you boys of summer in your ruin.
> Man in his maggot's barren.
> And boys are full and foreign in the pouch.
> I am the man your father was.
> We are the sons of flint and pitch.
> O see the poles are kissing as they cross.

Each of the lines is end-stopped; nowhere does

Thomas' propensity for short independent images reveal itself more clearly. As usual the question is, what are these separate "adventures" and what unifying idea gives them their coherence? Line 1, obviously a close parallel of the first line of the poem, summarizes the complaint against the boys in part I. Shorn of all particulars, the complaint is concentrated in the symbols "summer" and "ruin," with stress on the negative pole. Line 2 is negative, but without the saving implication of the positive pole. Man is in "his maggot," his fleshly body. His flesh, his mortal dross, is a maggot because a maggot symbolizes the corruption and decay to which the flesh is subject. It is the man of winter; his barrenness means there will be no blowing back. Thus, we have the larger contrast in the poem: polarity (challenging) versus non-polarity (stagnation). The boys are half-destructive, but their destruction is essential to the life-cycle. Their polarity is expressed again in line 3. They are "full," indicating their potentiality for good; they are "foreign," which summarizes all their antagonism. The pouch, whether marsupial or scrotal, is polar, containing these opposites.

By all traditional esthetic canons, it is now far too late for the "I" observer to start playing a dramatic role in the poem; yet we have the line "I am the man your father was." The most sensible paraphrase of the line seems to be: I am the kind of man your father used to be. But this does not say much about the boys or the father, or the "I" for that matter. This failure on the literal level forces us immediately to the level of symbolic presentation. The "I" seems to be present as a convenient digit for constructing a symbolic structure. The "I" relates himself to the two generations older and younger, fixing himself midway in the life-span, thus giving the symbolic assertion: two poles (boys and father) with the central point (the "I"), a meeting point of youth and age. This, at least, is the conclusion toward which the poem is leading. "Flint and pitch," two extremes, spark and unite in the boys. And the poles kiss in the last line. Here Thomas would probably be thinking of the common sign for a kiss, a cross — but also, one can be sure, of the Christian connotation. Where everlasting life came at the moment of death, the positive and negative forces in the universe might be considered to have crossed most significantly.

This last line of the poem is a climax prepared for by the previous last lines:

(I) O see the pulse of summer in the ice.
(II) O see the poles of promise in the boys.
(III) O see the poles are kissing as they cross.

These key lines are linked by reiteration of sound, which helps to pull the poem together. Mutability in its traditional destructive aspects was the subject of part I until the end when the dual nature of destruction was hinted at. Part II stated directly the superiority of challenge over stagnation. The boys denied everything, and thus were partly creative. Part III recapitulated the previous ideas and expressed the dynamic balance between polar tensions, growth and decay, in each instant of experience. No wonder Thomas picked out this poem for the beginning of his first volume. It is the fullest statement of his basic view of the universe as a war of conflicting forces.

Since his own poetry is written in a warring of images, the poem also sums up his poetic method, implying the unity between poetry and life.

[4]

Thomas' early poetry has not appealed to those who like poetry to be *about something*. They have assumed that because it is difficult to see any central subject the poems do not communicate intelligibly but employ a kind of automatic writing. But we have seen, with this first poem at least, that Thomas does make a coherent assertion in spite of disparate imagery — indeed, because of disparate imagery. *I see the boys of summer* is a poem *about* polarity, and the disparate imagery demonstrates the extremes of the polar opposites. Direct statements do appear in the poem: "Seasons must be challenged," "O see the poles of promise," and so on. We shouldn't distrust these statements of theme just because they are direct and therefore exceptional. We might wish for more. We would certainly feel more secure in our interpretations generally if Thomas had divulged precisely what he meant to say in at least one poem. Then we could see how the interpretation and the poem fit together; we wouldn't have to work it all by deduction. Actually there is one such case. In a letter to Vernon Watkins, Thomas encloses *Into her Lying Down Head* and tells what it is *about:*

It is a poem about modern love. For some reason, I wrote a note under the poem in my copybook: All over the world love is being betrayed as always, and a million years have not calmed the uncalculated ferocity of each betrayal or the terrible loneliness afterwards. Man is denying his partner man or woman and whores with the whole night, begetting a monstrous brood; one day the brood will not die when the day comes but will hang on to the breast and the parts and squeeze his partner out of bed.[10]

Even in his paraphrase, Thomas cannot stop being the poet; he uses further images instead of explanations. The point, however, is clear: much of our love-making is insincere lust, devastating to human sensibility and ending in hatred. The three-part poem is long and complicated, but the paraphrase reassures us that it has coherence, that it is *about* something.

I

Into her lying down head
His enemies entered bed,
Under the encumbered eyelid,
Through the rippled drum of the hair-buried ear;
And Noah's rekindled now unkind dove
Flew man-bearing there.
Last night in a raping wave
Whales unreined from the green grave
In fountains of origin gave up their love,
Along her innocence glided
Juan aflame and savagely young King Lear,
Queen Catherine howling bare
And Samson drowned in his hair,
The colossal intimacies of silent
Once seen strangers or shades on a stair;

There the dark blade and wanton sighing her down
To a haycock couch and the scythes of his arms
   Rode and whistled a hundred times
   Before the crowing morning climbed;
Man was the burning England she was sleep-walking,
  and the enamouring island
 Made her limbs blind by luminous charms,
Sleep to a newborn sleep in a swaddling loin-leaf
  stroked and sang
 And his runaway beloved childlike laid in the
  acorned sand.

Once it is known that the "enemies" entering the
marriage bed are the fantasy figures with which the
partner is unfaithful (the poem concentrates on the
woman's infidelities), the disparate images can all be
interpreted in terms of this third party; their profu-
sion expresses the enormity of the tragedy. Noah's
dove of peace is bred dialectically from "enemies."
It is a dove with a difference, now "unkind" and
"man-bearing," bringing the rival instead of an olive
branch. The whales that come in a "raping wave"
are also in the *Ballad of the Long-legged Bait*, which
is close to this poem in date and in the use of violent
imagery for sexual union. The unlikely combination
of Juan, young King Lear, Queen Catherine, and
Samson, added to the "strangers or shades on a stair,"
serves by its very unlikeliness to emphasize the pro-
miscuity. Lines 16-19, where the "blade" (a sharp
fellow?) "dark" and "wanton" rides and whistles,
expresses the sexual act by means of hay-cutting puns.
In the last lines of part I, the woman is being made
love to by the whole island of England ("Circe's
swinish, coiling island" in the first printing); this

population of charming males "blinds" her limbs,
strokes and sings and lays her in the sand.

II

There where a numberless tongue
　　　　Wound their room with a male moan,
　His faith around her flew undone
And darkness hung the walls with baskets of snakes,
A furnace-nostrilled column-membered
　　　　　　Super-or-near man
　　　　Resembling to her dulled sense
　　　　The thief of adolescence,
Early imaginary half remembered
　　　　Oceanic lover alone
Jealousy cannot forget for all her sakes,
　　　　Made his bad bed in her good
　　　　Night, and enjoyed as he would.
Crying, white gowned, from the middle moonlit
　　stages
　　　　Out to the tiered and hearing tide,
Close and far she announced the theft of the heart
In the taken body at many ages,
　　　　Trespasser and broken bride
　　　　Celebrating at her side
All blood-signed assailings and vanished marriages in
　　which he had no lovely part
　　　　Nor could share, for his pride, to the least
Mutter and foul wingbeat of the solemnizing
　　nightpriest
　Her holy unholy hours with the always anonymous
　　beast.

Part II continues the theme: while countless
male tongues (like baskets of snakes) moan around
the bedroom, betraying her infidelities, she confesses
to the night all the "vanished marriages" in which

her husband had no part. The rival is here pictured as a superman, "column-membered," a raping image out of her past, the thief of adolescence, a trespasser,[11] and an anonymous beast.

The "monstrous brood" of Thomas' paraphrase, the progeny of the myriad promiscuities, is only hinted at in the poem as we have it; and the picture of their forcing the partners out of bed is material enough for a part IV. The implication of conception is present in part III, but the tone is not so malicious as one might expect.

III

Two sand grains together in bed,
Head to heaven-circling head,
Singly lie with the whole wide shore,
The covering sea their nightfall with no names;
And out of every domed and soil-based shell
One voice in chains declaims
The female, deadly, and male
Libidinous betrayal,
Golden dissolving under the water veil.
A she bird sleeping brittle by
Her lover's wings that fold to-morrow's flight,
Within the nested treefork
Sings to the treading hawk
Carrion, paradise, chirrup my bright yolk.
A blade of grass longs with the meadow,
A stone lies lost and locked in the lark-high hill.
Open as to the air to the naked shadow
O she lies alone and still,
Innocent between two wars,
With the incestuous secret brother in the seconds to
perpetuate the stars,
A man torn up mourns in the sole night.

And the second comers, the severers, the enemies
   from the deep
Forgotten dark, rest their pulse and bury their dead
   in her faithless sleep.

The male, female, libidinous, and deadly betrayal
is over, dissolving under the water veil. A seashore
image and then a bird image express the resting
period after the war of sex. The "bright yolk" and
"the seconds to perpetuate the stars" suggest conception, and the last line confirms it with the reference
to burying the dead. Thomas in other places implies
that the husband has much less to do with conception
than the wife and their ancestors. In the *Ballad of
the Long-legged Bait* it is "his fathers" who "cling to
the hand of the girl" and announce that "Time is
bearing another son." In *A grief ago*, the ancestors
again preside over conception: "Let her inhale her
dead, through seed and solid / Draw in their seas."
Thomas' view of childbirth, as we have seen with the
summer children in their mothers, brings out the cruel
antagonism between parent and offspring. In *It is the
sinners' dust-tongued bell*, the parents are a "plagued
groom and bride" and the child "the urchin grief."
At best, conception is the beginning of suffering; and
in *Into her Lying Down Head* it is the infidelities of
the marriage bed that produce the offspring. The
"enemies from the deep forgotten dark" create the
new enemy. So that the woman's sleep as well as her
loving is "faithless" in that she has conceived a grief
and a rival.

The periodical publication of the poem had a
more direct reference to the paraphrase's "monstrous
brood":

Damned damned go down or caress to death
   the sun-sized bridal bed's cruellest brood.

In the draft that Thomas had sent to Watkins earlier, this long line had made an even more direct statement of the horror produced by infidelity:

The filth and secret of death is sweeter with
   the sun than these inconstancies.

Thomas wondered if the line wasn't too "prosy."[12] The revision was thus deliberately more "obscure," as was the final rewriting:

O she lies alone and still,
Innocent between two wars,
With the incestuous secret brother in the
   seconds to perpetuate the stars.

The long line is here simpler in form, yet more taxing: the "brother" seems more significant than the "enemies." Has the man found kinship with his rival? If so, Thomas' paraphrase does not fully apply to the poem as it now stands.

We have gone far enough into this major poem to see that behind the complexity is a central assertion which only such complexity can fully communicate to the poet's satisfaction. Thomas' paraphrase of the poem is confirmation that our effort to find coherence in these difficult poems is warranted. What finally is left to trouble us is whether or not the intricacy is as valuable to the reader as it apparently is to the poet. Thomas' narrative of disparate images has seemed to some readers a mere play of empty forms. Donald Davie coined the word "pseudo-syntax" to denote a sentence that only *appears* to be communicating meaning but isn't, and has suggested that Thomas' "pseudo-syntax" is "radically vicious."[13] If Thomas' image-narrative only *appeared* to be telling about events, we should probably have to agree with Davie. But Thomas once said in a letter, "Try to Think in Things," and has elsewhere, as we have seen, asserted his desire to have his images taken seriously on a literal level. Any poet describes imaginary events. Some of Thomas' are especially hard to imagine; yet he asks us to do so. When he writes in *Altarwise by owl-light*, "Time tracks the sound of shape on man and cloud," he is depicting an event. Time (personified) tracks sound (like a sound track), sound which is really the expression of shape or form. Man and cloud are given their existence within time, as though they were ticked into shape. The line in the context of sonnet VII is another expression of mortality. The particular adventure in this line may not be very comfortable to contemplate, but Davie will not have it as an event at all:

> The verb "tracks" is completely devoid of meaning. What appears to be narrative ("Time," the agent, transfers energy through "tracks" to the object "sound") is in fact an endless series of copulas: "Time is tracking which is sound which is shape . . ." and so on. That the metaphors could in fact be broken down into successive meanings is irrelevant; even when the breaking down has been done for us, we cannot hold on to it when we return to reading the poem.[14]

In stating the problem in terms of the endurance

demanded of the reader, Davie has raised the issue of Thomas' poetry in its proper form. Such a line as the above is pseudo-syntax if we find ourselves unable to take the event seriously. In the words of John Bayley, the critic who has gone perhaps most searchingly into the problem of Thomas' obscurity:

> The critical uncertainty which must still be felt about Thomas' real status as a poet arises from the fact that we still do not know whether language is capable of what he tried to do with it; or rather whether the consciousness of the receiver can adapt itself to such a variety of linguistic uses and such a multiplicity of verbal stimuli.

Bayley adds: "Probably it can."[15] And one reader, at least, A. D. S. Fowler, is willing to challenge Davie's specific accusation:

> On five lines wrenched from Dylan Thomas's "Now stamp the Lord's Prayer," the only pathological specimen he examines in any detail, Davie puts forward only unsympathetic and unsupported reiterations that the "syntax cannot mime, as it offers to do, a movement of the mind . . . these sentences that seem to drive forward in time through their verbs in fact do no such thing. The verb 'tracks' is completely devoid of meaning." . . . One is irritated into replying: "The verb 'tracks' is *not* devoid of meaning: prove that it is." Thomas's syntax is not shown to be defective, except by criteria which would condemn equally Sidney,

Daniel, Milton, and, indeed, most of the poetry we value.[16]

With this positive note one can concur, if only on the grounds of personal experience. The "multiplicity of verbal stimuli" in Thomas' poetry does become easier to handle and more rewarding as time goes on. The "variety of linguistic uses" becomes less bewildering when one can see a certain basic methodology. Every image in Thomas has to be taken on its own merits and it is impossible to say, for instance, that Thomas is likely at any particular time to be employing a proverbial expression, a Biblical reference, or a Freudian symbol. These kinds of images occur often, but so do a hundred other kinds. The two broad lines of approach that we have found useful with the poems discussed so far are, first, each image in a poem is best looked upon as isolated, having its own internal logic and only superficial associations with adjacent imagery on the narrative level. We have seen how casually an image is born out of another, but this casualness and perhaps verbal similarity should not deceive us into thinking that the new image is not entirely new. The way to understand these images, if we are to read them in the spirit in which they were written, is to treat them first of all as literal events. Second, the full significance of a poem will be in the literal narrative plus the central concept inherent in the symbolic power of the wording. The generality of the symbolized concept is determined by the range of the imagery in the poem; the images receive their deeper significance, and the poem its coherence, from that generality.

[5]

By the time of *Deaths and Entrances* (1946)
Thomas had developed a more open and relaxed style
in a good many of his poems. The rigorousness of
our own approach can consequently be tempered.
Thomas gives us a more realistic setting in these
poems, more of a world we recognize. There is disparate imagery, but the assertion to which the images
are attached is usually clear. Thomas was aware that
he had become a more accessible poet:

> It is impossible to be too clear. I am trying
> for more clarity now. At first I thought it
> enough to leave an impression of sound and
> feeling and let the meaning seep in later, but
> since I have been giving these broadcasts
> and reading other men's poetry as well as
> my own, I find it better to have more mean-
> ing at first reading.[17]

The war thrust Thomas into contact with a wider
audience through his work in films and broadcasting.
But the war itself, as a subject, demanded a wider
audience. Thomas' reaction to the war was personal,
but the subject was public, and he found a new
authoritative voice with which to proclaim it. Typ-
ical of the new poem is *A Refusal to Mourn the
Death, by Fire, of a Child in London* (published
1945), whose title announces what it is *about*.

> Never until the mankind making
> Bird beast and flower
> Fathering and all humbling darkness
> Tells with silence the last light breaking

And the still hour
Is come of the sea tumbling in harness

And I must enter again the round
Zion of the water bead
And the synagogue of the ear of corn
Shall I let pray the shadow of a sound
Or sow my salt seed
In the least valley of sackcloth to mourn

The majesty and burning of the child's death.
I shall not murder
The mankind of her going with a grave truth
Nor blaspheme down the stations of the breath
With any further
Elegy of innocence and youth.

Deep with the first dead lies London's daughter,
Robed in the long friends,
The grains beyond age, the dark veins of her
    mother,
Secret by the unmourning water
Of the riding Thames.
After the first death, there is no other.

"Never until I die shall I say a word or shed a tear of mourning for this dead child." We don't here reach the main assertion through a series of "adventures." The assertion is clear; we merely have to recognize the understatement. In refusing to mourn, the poet utilizes the language and sentiments of intense mourning. His refusal to be elegiac becomes a great elegy.

The poem is not without its own set of difficulties; for instance, the protracted compound adjective stretched over the first three lines:

> Never until the mankind making
> Bird beast and flower
> Fathering and all humbling darkness.

With these run-on lines, a contrast to the end-stopped lines of the *18 Poems*, we are forced to pay attention to the individual word before, and momentarily quite apart from, the meaning of the sentence as a whole. The device works. The darkness is (1) mankind-making, (2) bird-, beast-, and flower-fathering, and (3) all-humbling. It was there at the beginning and will be there at the end. The way the poetry holds apart the "making" and the "humbling" mimicks the life-span of man and the world. Again, an adjective such as "round" comes out very strongly when broken from its noun:

> And I must enter again the round
> Zion of the water bead.

"The round zion" is the static paradise to which man returns. By stressing the circularity, the poet suggests other associations: the life cycle, a zero, the world in the waterdrop.

As though the poem were a discursive essay, the initial statement of refusal to mourn is followed by the reason for refusing:

> I shall not murder
> The mankind of her going with a grave truth
> Nor blaspheme down the stations of the breath
> With any further
> Elegy of innocence and youth.

The immoderateness of "murder" confirms the poet's high seriousness. To mourn would be to murder the child twice (we assume what we are not told: that the child was killed in an air raid) because all the words available are necessarily inadequate, over-solemn truths or thumbed elegies. The language here is loaded with connotations. The "mankind of her going" — a strange construction — communicates the worldwide implications of the child's death. The "stations of the breath," echoing "stations of the Cross," expresses the poet's resolution to keep his art sacred.

> Deep with the first dead lies London's daughter,
> Robed in the long friends,
> The grains beyond age, the dark veins of her
>   mother,
> Secret by the unmourning water
> Of the riding Thames.
> After the first death, there is no other.

This last stanza gives a further reason for the refusal to mourn. The earth with its dust and immortality has welcomed the child like an old friend or mother. This is not a Christian heaven; the round zion of the water bead is part of a river that does not mourn. But "after the first death, there is no other"; the consolation is that there is not another death to face.

The fact that the poem ends with an unadorned explanatory assertion shows how far Thomas has come in his aim to give more meaning at first reading. The meaning we look for in subsequent readings is, in a sense, extra. The ultimate significance is in the full power and depth of certain striking words. Take for another example the climactic stanzas of *A Winter's Tale* (also 1945):

> For the bird lay bedded
> In a choir of wings, as though she slept or died,
> And the wings glided wide and he was hymned
>   and wedded,
> And through the thighs of the engulfing bride,
> The woman breasted and the heaven headed
>
> Bird, he was brought low,
> Burning in the bride bed of love, in the whirl-
> Pool at the wanting centre, in the folds
> Of paradise, in the spun bud of the world.
> And she rose with him flowering in her melting
>   snow.

The image of the she-bird is not one of those short-lived images of the early poems that immediately fades and breeds another, different image. On the contrary, it provides the central core of the poem. The poem has its literal level: during a snowfall, a she-bird comes to the man sitting by his fire in the valley farmhouse. There are very real "puffed birds hopping and hunting" in the poem; and this climax is Leda and the Swan in reverse. But the final meaning is in the symbolic connotations of certain words used to describe the she-bird and the lover; for instance, "whirlpool," which in becoming two words (whirl- / Pool) communicates both destruction and the great energy of life at its highest point of surrender. By means of such words, the poet imparts to the reader his sense of the mystical unity of love and death. It should also be clear from this and the above examples that there is frustration in trying to anticipate or tabulate the ways in which Thomas puts extra meaning into his words. In the next chapter we go as far as we can in identifying and describing Thomas' special vocabulary of process words. But for the most part there is no sure scheme. If "whirl- / Pool" gives added meaning to *A Winter's Tale*, the poem itself has made it possible for the word to do so. One relies on the context and on the dictionary meaning of the words.

Chapter III

Process Poems

*"To others caught
Between black and white"*

Thomas' inscription on
the August 1933 Notebook

HERE IN ITS SIMPLEST TERMS is the duality of the world portrayed in *I see the boys of summer* and the larger part of *18 Poems*. It is convenient to term the poems that treat this struggle between black and white "process poems." Process is the subject — obviously so in *A process in the weather of the heart*, written two months before *I see the boys of summer:*

A process in the weather of the heart
Turns damp to dry; the golden shot
Storms in the freezing tomb.
A weather in the quarter of the veins
Turns night to day; blood in their suns
Lights up the living worm.

A process in the eye forwarns
The bones of blindness; and the womb
Drives in a death as life leaks out.

A darkness in the weather of the eye
Is half its light; the fathomed sea
Breaks on unangled land.

57

The seed that makes a forest of the loin
Forks half its fruit; and half drops down,
Slow in a sleeping wind.

A weather in the flesh and bone
Is damp and dry; the quick and dead
Move like two ghosts before the eye.

A process in the weather of the world
Turns ghost to ghost; each mothered child
Sits in their double shade.
A process blows the moon into the sun,
Pulls down the shabby curtains of the skin;
And the heart gives up its dead.

This smaller poem says much the same thing as *I see
the boys of summer*. When the "golden shot storms
in the freezing tomb," the boys of summer could
very well be at work "denying" the coldness of the
tomb with "golden shot," a metaphor for sunlight.
Again much of the action occurs inside the human
body. Night becomes day inside the veins; it is as
though each corpuscle of the veins were a sun whose
blood lights up the body (or one specifically worm-
like part of the body). Again a counterpoise is main-
tained between positive and negative images. The sun
imagery of the first six lines calls up the reference
to blindness in the seventh. This poem has more
formal statements of theme: "A darkness in the
weather of the eye is half its light"; and the imagery
that expresses the duality is more clear-cut: the division between light and dark is simply represented,
for instance, by the two opposites, deep sea and un-
fished land. Half of the sexual seed (from the pubic
forest) "forks," which is a positive, vigorous action;

while half drops down during sleep. Life and death are two ghosts or images, each taking on the other's appearance; every individual is under their sway. The last three lines of the poem signify the end of the dual process in death.

Besides general similarities, much of the actual wording of this poem duplicates that of *I see the boys of summer*. Notably, the word "weather" recalls

> I see the summer children in their mothers
> Split up the brawned womb's weathers.

"Weather" is an effective "process" word. A speaker in Shakespeare says: "It is foul weather in us all, good sir, when you are cloudy." In Thomas, this equation of the sky with internal states has come a good deal further. One is hardly permitted to think of the sky any more, but of some seemingly no less physical atmospheric conditions existing within the flesh and bone of the body. If the inner processes of life and death are contained in the words "damp" and "dry," then the state of the processes at any time will logically be "the weather," the two weathers vying for dominance. The very strangeness of the rare plural "weathers"[1] and "*a* weather" (as opposed to *the* weather) makes these forms effective in signifying the strange forces beneath the surface of things. Several other words particularly suited to expressing process are common to the two poems, and occur elsewhere more or less coextensive with the poems whose subject is process; so that one can begin to talk of a "process vocabulary" as characterizing a "process poem."

The word "process" itself appears only four times in Thomas' poetry — in the poem we have been discussing. Process words are those that offer a good alternative for that key word. "Tides" is one such word. Like "weathers," the word is rare in the plural outside of Thomas' process vocabulary. We are accustomed to speak of "*the* tide," there being usually only one tide at a time. "Tides," as Thomas uses it, communicates a strange sense of the habitual rising and falling motions underlying universal flux.

> Where no sea runs, the waters of the heart
> Push in their tides.

These tides of *Light breaks where no sun shines*, like the tides in which the boys of summer drown the "cargoed apples" and with which they "choke the deserts," are more than a seaside phenomenon; they are the medium by which forces of change can be imagined as operating. In the words of *Before I knocked*, they are "tides that never touch the shores." In the same way, "eye" in the singular is often a process word. We see through our "eyes" (plural); the "eye" in Thomas is rather the globe within which forces of light and darkness clash. So that in our prototype process poem we find, "a process in the eye" and "a darkness in the weather of the eye"; and in *Light breaks where no sun shines*, "the secret of the soil grows through the eye"; and so on. Not every "eye" need be a process "eye," nor all "tides" process "tides"; but a count of these words and others like them, blunt though a count may be as a critical instrument, is impressive. "Tides" occurs eight times in six of the *18 Poems*, and only twice in the remainder of the poems (more than three times the number of lines). The more commonplace "tide" doesn't occur at all in *18 Poems*, but eleven times elsewhere. The process word "eye" occurs thirteen times in ten of the *18 Poems*, once in *I, in my intricate image* (which poem might be counted as the nineteenth of the *18 Poems*), and only eleven times elsewhere. On the other hand, "eyes" occurs only four times in *18 Poems*, but forty times elsewhere. Some other characteristic process words, with the ratio of their relatively high concentration in *18 Poems* (plus the nineteenth), are flesh 21:16, ghost 27:17, bone 22:33, blood 23:33, fork 7:5, bud 4:2, force 3:0, womb 8:7, vein 7:7, root 7:7, oil 6:3, wax 3:1, matter 3:1, skin 3:2, dry 16:13, damp 6:1, weather(s) 13:12.[2]

Generally speaking, we can say that process vocabulary (which is to say the process poem as well) has disappeared by the outbreak of war. Thomas used the plural "weathers" for the last time in 1938; and in that year we see him deliberately forgoing "weather" as a process word. In March 1938 he sent to Vernon Watkins a rewritten draft of *Not from this anger* (originally 20 April 1933 in the notebooks), with the line: "In a land without weathers." The poem is chronologically a pre-process poem, and this attempt by Thomas to tap the deeper process level produced a noticeable strain. Watkins must have remarked on it, for on 1 April 1938 Thomas wrote: "Before your letter came, I had cut out the ubiquitous 'weather' from the anticlimactic poem, and am revising it all."[3] He didn't revise the whole poem, but he did cut out the "land without weathers," substituting the present line: "In a land strapped by hunger."

"Without weather" meant that the land was without the working processes of nature. "Strapped by hunger" gives the same idea: the land is desolate. But the word "hunger" operates in its own image for desolation, not relying on previous connections with process themes. One "weather" couldn't make a poem a process poem. At the same time, for those who have previously felt its force, some of the process connotation stays with the word in its later more conventional usage, for example in *Poem in October* (perhaps begun 1939; finished 1944):

> There I could marvel
> My birthday
> Away but the weather turned around.

Or in the *Ballad of the Long-legged Bait* (1941):

> The boat swims into the six-year weather.

The contexts support the extraordinary meaning, the vestigial notion of underlying processes. The very fact that we can talk of vestigial meaning shows how strongly established is the use of "weather" as a process word.

Perhaps no other word can we be so sure about. Whenever we want to make a generalization about Thomas' use of words, we run up against one overriding generalization: that his words rarely have exactly the same meaning twice. Each new occurrence in an image is likely to call forth a new significance from the range of a word's possible meanings. Thomas was not being fair to himself when he said:

> I agree that each of my earlier poems might
> appear to constitute a section from one long

> poem; that is because I was not successful in making a momentary peace with my images at the correct moment; images were left dangling over the formal limits, and dragged the poem into another.[4]

If it were strictly true that these early poems were all scoops from the same stream of images, then it would be easy to explicate one poem by means of another. The images, dangling over from one poem to the next, would be common to both, and doubly revealing. But we saw in the last chapter that Thomas' images, despite the ultimate similarity in thought content and a surface similarity of wording, are usually quite distinct from one another. And although we can identify certain words as "process" words, the actual use of such words is not as mechanical as a word count might suggest. They are not bricks, but clay blocks to be molded differently in each image. Such a word as "worm" (occurring in ten of the *18 Poems* and in only three later poems) is a good process block, witness "the wormy winter" in *Especially when the October wind* (1934 version); but it is used with a wide variety of denotative meanings by Thomas: (a) charnel worm, (b) parasitic worm, (c) phallic worm, (d) glowworm, (e) umbilical cord, (f) Satan, and (g) the common garden worm. Given this variety, in what respects can it be a called a process word? For one thing, in its different meanings it is very useful for making an image, which image gives us the process theme. But why should it be especially useful for making a process image? It is simply that the word, whatever it denotes in the image, cannot shake off its association with mortality.

If one's object is to communicate the idea of decay and death, one worm will perhaps do just as well as another; one gets variety of imagery within the single purpose.

On the other hand, Thomas did not perversely require that a word have a brand new meaning every time. Often when we suspect a rather extreme twist to a word, we find that the poet has moved in that direction elsewhere. "Man in his maggot" from *I see the boys of summer* is a case in point. We took "maggot" to indicate the man's flesh, his body. This occurrence of "maggot" is the last of seven (if we include those in the notebooks). It would be all to the good if the interpretation here were backed up by at least one of the seven. *Find meat on bones*, originally poem Forty Six in the February 1933 Notebook, has

> Rebel against the flesh and bone,
> The word of the blood, the wily skin,
> And the maggot no man can slay.

The rebellion here is against the body, the flesh and bone, blood and skin, and the "maggot," the symbol of decay, indicating the mortality of the whole body. We get even closer in poem Twenty Eight of the August 1933 Notebook, which begins

> Here lies the worm of man.

A dead man is speaking of himself lying under the ground, "worm" denoting the corpse itself. Thomas altered the line to: "Here lies the beast of man," which indicates that "worm" was roughly equivalent to "beast," the carcass of the man as opposed to his

soul. Thomas apparently shied away from the use
of "worm" here; six months later he did use the idea
in *I see the boys of summer*, pushing it a stage further:
"maggot" becomes the living body, barren in that
it presages its own death. These are far-fetched
images and readings; but two uncertainties, if they
are found to have been fetched in the same way, may
have the effect of increasing each other's certainty.[5]

[2]

The contending forces of growth and decay
find their natural expression in antithetical imagery,
one image posed against its opposite in imitation of
the balance of forces. The likelihood of antithesis in
a poem is a great help in explication. In *I see the boys
of summer* the line "Here break a kiss in no love's
quarry" had to be positive in order for the contraries
to even out properly — there was at least that expectation to go on. Other process poems set up similar
expectations in their rhetorical forms, notably *The
force that through the green fuse drives the flower*,
whose subtlety within antithesis is worth looking
into:

> The force that through the green fuse drives the
>   flower
> Drives my green age; that blasts the roots of trees
> Is my destroyer.
> And I am dumb to tell the crooked rose
> My youth is bent by the same wintry fever.

The force that drives the water through the
    rocks
Drives my red blood; that dries the mouthing
    streams
Turns mine to wax.
And I am dumb to mouth unto my veins
How at the mountain spring the same mouth
    sucks.

The hand that whirls the water in the pool
Stirs the quicksand; that ropes the blowing wind
Hauls my shroud sail.
And I am dumb to tell the hanging man
How of my clay is made the hangman's lime.

The lips of time leech to the fountain head;
Love drips and gathers, but the fallen blood
Shall calm her sores.
And I am dumb to tell a weather's wind
How time has ticked a heaven round the stars.

And I am dumb to tell the lover's tomb
How at my sheet goes the same crooked worm.

As usual we look first for the dialectic breeding of
imagery. The gunpowder conceit of the first line
(the flower seen as an explosion at the top of its
stem, the fuse) supplies the "blasts" of the second
line, which, however, utilizes the alternative meaning
of "blasts" in the blighting of the roots of trees. The
disease element is retained in "fever"; and "blasts"
is recalled in "wintry," a third connotation. This is
a curious kind of balancing effect. Besides the literal
narrative, there is non-discursive communication in
the placing and permutating of the symbolic words

within the stanza frame. This presentational mode is part of the stuff of poetry — part of its magic, if not its meaning proper. We are chiefly concerned with meaning; but we should acknowledge the role of such balanced symbols in supporting, though unobtrusively, the balanced import of the assertions. Take, as a specially striking example, the "crooked worm" of the last line echoing the "crooked rose" of the first refrain. Such repetition binds a poem. An "unbound" poem gives quite a different sensation, which must affect the meaning in some way, though it seems impossible to speak of the effect in any but the vaguest terms. As a matter of fact, the link here has a direct bearing on meaning. The rose is "crooked" because it contains a "crooked worm." Derek Stanford is right to think of Blake's *The Sick Rose*.[6] Thomas surely had Blake in mind when he wrote the first draft in the August 1933 Notebook:

> The force that through the green fuse drives the
>   flower
> Drives my green age; that blasts the roots of trees
> Is my destroyer.
> And I am dumb to tell the eaten rose
> How at my sheet goes the same crookèd worm,
> And dumb to holla thunder to the skies
> How at my cloths flies the same central storm.

We still have something of Blake's "howling storm" in the "wintry fever." The "worm" is split from the "rose"; but Blake's images now span the poem and the connection is telling.

Antithetical form is very clear in the first stanza: the force that, on the one hand, brings the flowering of youth causes, on the other hand, destruction, which is then emphasized in the refrain. The second stanza repeats the form:

> The force that drives the water through the
>   rocks
> Drives my red blood; that dries the mouthing
>   streams
> Turns mine to wax.

Again, the two forces, growth and destruction, operate both in nature and in the individual. The second refrain continues the theme, with a slight variation:

> I am dumb to mouth unto my veins
> How at the mountain spring the same mouth
>   sucks.

Exactly parallel wording would have given, as the first refrain:

> I am dumb to mouth unto the spring
> How at my veins the same mouth sucks.

Besides avoiding exact repetition, the reversal adds an increment of meaning through a play on the word "mouth." "Mouthing streams" are streams at the mouth, the estuary. The mouth sucking at the mountain spring can be thought of as the estuary, sucking down the whole course of the stream into the sea. The force that drives the water through the rocks is the same as that which sucks it in at the mouth: in short, the creating and destroying forces are identical. This same mouth, the estuary, sucks at the veins. The poet is leading up to a leech image in stanza four, but here the image is of the bloodstream, the stream of life, beginning in youth, with time slowly sucking away vitality, pulling toward the estuary, death. The force that drives the blood also dries it; the force of youth pulls one on to age. The same idea is represented differently in the next stanza:

> The hand that whirls the water in the pool
> Stirs the quicksand; that ropes the blowing wind
> Hauls my shroud sail.

The force that whirls the water (positive action) stirs quicksand (betokening death). The force blows both the ship of life and the ship of death. The two forces are one.

Another extraordinary effect is achieved here. Imbedded in each side of the equation is a tacit counter-assertion. The hand whirling the pool brings up the idea of whirlpool, as much a symbol of destruction as the quicksand, which in turn has the under-suggestion of sands of life in the positive element "quick." And, similarly, to rope the blowing wind suggests a binding, constraining force; while the hauling of the sail, shroud or no, is very active, gives the impression of a voyage under way. These echoes, seemingly subversive to the image containing them, really support the theme, the point that the life and death forces are the same. When $A = B$, there is every reason for seeing B in A and A in B. Is this same kind of two-way cross current in the refrain?

> And I am dumb to tell the hanging man
> How of my clay is made the hangman's lime.

We certainly wouldn't see it unless we were looking for it. The poet's mortal clay is not only dead but is the receptor for dead flesh, doubly dead. Though the positive doesn't have much chance here, "lime" no doubt came down from "quicksand" (via quick-lime) and shares the same implication of "quick." The lime pit is, in a sense, cleansing. Positive effects can, according to Thomas' way of looking at things, come out of the macabre. This is the point of the next image:

> The lips of time leech to the fountain head;
> Love drips and gathers, but the fallen blood
> Shall calm her sores.

Time is a leech, which sucks at the fountain head of Love, making a sore wound. But the loss of blood, in keeping with archaic lore, is beneficial. The refrain of this stanza makes the same assertion of unexpected good coming from evil:

> And I am dumb to tell a weather's wind
> How time has ticked a heaven round the stars.

"Heaven" must be positive; Thomas would not use it ironically here.[7] When Time, usually the agent of destruction, ticks a *heaven* round the stars, it is un-expected, but that is the whole point — positive comes out of the usually negative.

As in certain lines of *I see the boys of summer* we have again the Christian doctrine of the fortunate fall. We cannot escape the Christian connotation in "heaven" and "fallen blood." "Fountain head," too, is very New Testament. Thomas elsewhere calls Christ "all glory's sawbones" (sonnet VIII), and "leech" is another name for doctor, Christ the doctor who saves us all, saves us from the "weather's wind" of mortality. This is not to say that we have here a

Christian poem. Thomas exploits the Christian concept of life coming out of death, just as he exploits medieval medicine, just as, indeed, he exploits the personal lament. How easy it would have been, were this poem truly personal, to have said "calm *my* sores" instead of "calm her [love's] sores." The personal references earlier are anonymous; the real subject is the idea of contending forces in nature and the vital role of destruction. Of course, the forces do cause dismay, and regret is the dominant response to the world of flux. The refrains communicate this tone, which is summed up in the final isolated couplet:

> And I am dumb to tell the lover's tomb
> How at my sheet goes the same crooked worm.

The poet is expressing his identity with the dead lover, knowing himself to be mortal, the worm already at his sheet as though it were his shroud. The pathos here seems to set at nought the "heaven" of the previous lines. At the end of his celebration of the dual processes in nature, the poet emphasizes the negative. We have learned to expect antithetical statements in a process poem, but we cannot be too stern if the poet eschews perfect regularity. Each poem works out the antithesis in a way organic to itself. It is natural that this poem should end at its most elegiac. The poem is more than a bare statement about forces. Our abstracting the conceptual meaning is not an effort to reduce the poem's stature, but an effort to find the framework of absolute coherence without which the images are merely suggestive. The poem is, of course, all its constituent elements, all the applicable connotations and symbolic implications, including the elegiac tone. But the poem's "motivating center," as Thomas once put it, is the *idea* of the unity of contrary forces. And antithetical structure is one of the chief means of finding in the "womb of war" this center, this "momentary peace."

[4]

Reserved for separate treatment are a small group of process poems that have the specific subject, dreams. *Our eunuch dreams* is the clearest of them. Indeed, it is gratifying to see how reasonable one of the "obscure" *18 Poems* can be. It is meticulously paragraphed in four sections, and it asserts the sensible values of the working world. One thing makes it, and the other dream poems, extraordinary: the precise nature of the indictment of the world of dreams.

I

Our eunuch dreams, all seedless in the light,
Of light and love, the tempers of the heart,
Whack their boys' limbs,
And, winding-footed in their shawl and sheet,
Groom the dark brides, the widows of the night
Fold in their arms.

The shades of girls, all flavoured from their
   shrouds,
When sunlight goes are sundered from the
   worm,
The bones of men, the broken in their beds,
By midnight pulleys that unhouse the tomb.

II

In this our age the gunman and his moll,
Two one-dimensioned ghosts, love on a reel,
Strange to our solid eye,
And speak their midnight nothings as they swell;
When cameras shut they hurry to their hole
Down in the yard of day.

They dance between their arclamps and our
    skull,
Impose their shots, throwing the nights away;
We watch the show of shadows kiss or kill,
Flavoured of celluloid give love the lie.

The first two parts give the two worlds: first, dreams,
and then day-dreams, which is what the movies
amount to, in Thomas' view here. The dreams are
personified as ghosts rising nightly from their graves;
their actions are sexual and "flavoured of the shroud."
The "flavour" of celluloid is the same: sex and death.
The poet is driven to ask: Can either of these two
be the real world?

III

Which is the world? Of our two sleepings,
    which
Shall fall awake when cures and their itch
Raise up this red-eyed earth?
Pack off the shapes of daylight and their starch,
The sunny gentlemen, the Welshing rich,
Or drive the night-geared forth.

The photograph is married to the eye,
Grafts on its bride one-sided skins of truth;
The dream has sucked the sleeper of his faith
That shrouded men might marrow as they fly.

Movies are cheating (welshing), dreams are equally deceiving. The question is a rhetorical one; neither of these two worlds will hold true in the world of daylight.

IV

This is the world: the lying likeness of
Our strips of stuff that tatter as we move
Loving and being loth;
The dream that kicks the buried from their sack
And lets their trash be honoured as the quick.
This is the world. Have faith.

For we shall be a shouter like the cock,
Blowing the old dead back; our shots shall smack
The image from the plates;
And we shall be fit fellows for a life,
And who remain shall flower as they love,
Praise to our faring hearts.

In saying "This is the world" about movies and dreams, the poet is being sarcastic. "Have faith" is the turning point. The last section is a statement of positive action: the dreams are to be blown back, the screen figures shot at, and the values of waking life asserted.[8]

The full significance of *Our eunuch dreams* and its possibly over-optimistic ending is best seen through the perspective of three allied poems. The opening lines of *When once the twilight locks no longer* describe the birth and babyhood of the "I" of the poem, using sea imagery for the liquids of the womb and breast:

When once the twilight locks no longer
Locked in the long worm of my finger
Nor damned the sea that sped about my fist,
The mouth of time sucked, like a sponge,
The milky acid on each hinge,
And swallowed dry the waters of the breast.

When the galactic sea was sucked
And all the dry seabed unlocked,
I sent my creature scouting on the globe.

Then follows the images of the child's exploration of himself, realizing and celebrating the world of daylight by holding "a little sabbath with the sun." However, the early version of this poem in the August 1933 Notebook has none of these images of exploration, but takes us immediately into the world of sleep. The day is hardly introduced before the night comes to destroy it:

When the galactic sea was sucked
And all the dry sea bed unlocked,
Rose the dry ghost of night to suck the day;
No hyleg but the Sleeper's star
Shone on this globe of bone and hair,
No star but sleep's was nodding in the sky.

Then follow six stanzas of nightmare images, which were whittled down for the corresponding stanzas of the final version coming after the exploratory lines. The last stanza of the draft version intensifies the connection between sleeping, dreaming, and death; and, significantly, leaves us still inside the sleeper's world:

There is no sweetness in the dead
I feel not in my sleeping blood;

> Then sleep and dream, sleeps dreams and dies;
> When once the twilight locks no longer
> Locked in the long worm of my finger
> I did unlock the Sleeper's eyes.

Ending thus, the early version shows itself to be entirely an exposé of the degrading aspects of dreams. So that when we come to the last two stanzas of the poem as printed we can see them in a much surer light. The next to last stanza recapitulates the poem: first the womb and nursing stages, then the exploration of the infant into the world of actuality, and finally a summary of the consequences of falling asleep.

> When once the twilight screws were turned,
> And mother milk was stiff as sand,
> I sent my own ambassador to light;
> By trick or chance he fell asleep
> And conjured up a carcass shape
> To rob me of my fluids in his heart.

The dead appear and rob the dreamer of "fluids." The poem is about the horror of dreams; and also, in the last stanza of the final version, about the joyful release into the waking world:

> Awake, my sleeper, to the sun,
> A worker in the morning town,
> And leave the poppied pickthank where he lies;
> The fences of the light are down,
> All but the briskest riders thrown,
> And worlds hang on the trees.

These are lines added later. Again, as in *Our eunuch dreams*, the poet's second thoughts were to emphasize the positive aspects of living.

The third dream poem, *I fellowed sleep*, takes us almost immediately into the world of sleep with which the previous two poems have made us familiar. The geography of the sleeper's journey is rather more complicated here because it is really two journeys from two separate draft poems in the August 1933 Notebook: (1) Thirty One, a short pessimistic poem, very much in the dream-death category, and (2) Twenty Two, a visionary poem, which gives us a heaven not a nightmare. Without knowing these early drafts we might find it difficult to see that the change in location in stanza four of the published poem involves a spiritual change to optimism. Dreaming, then, is an important matter to Thomas. When he says, "These are but dreaming men," he really is talking about dreams and not about some remoter subject, a subject which, naturally, one cannot grasp, because it doesn't exist. And the optimistic ending to all these three poems means that it is important to him that we should "breathe" in "the living air."

The clue to the importance of dreams is given in the early draft of *From love's first fever to her plague*, a poem which is a fairly straightforward account of an individual's development through different stages from conception to adolescence. Symbolic of the kind of experience in each period, a numerical value increases with increasing awareness: one, two, four, and then a jump to a million. The last line gives a twist to the conceit: "One sun, one manna, warmed and fed." With this glance back at a supposed single source of life-power, the poem as we have it ends satisfactorily. In its manuscript version, however, the poem continues with a description of youth, the stage that the poem has brought us to:

> Now that drugged youth is waking from its
>   stupor,
> The nervous hand rehearsing on the thigh
> Acts with a woman, one sum remains in cipher;
> Five senses and the frozen brain
> Are one with wind, and itching in the sun.

A hand on the thigh rehearsing acts with a woman — this can only be interpreted as onanism. The numerical conceit is used to express the nullity of the act. In cutting out these depressing lines Thomas produced, again, a more optimistic poem. By leaving them in the notebooks, however, he has given the key to the other dream poems. It is in the same stage of youth, reached by the end of the second stanza of *When once the twilight locks no longer*, that the hero of that poem falls asleep:

> But when the stars, assuming shape,
> Drew in his eyes the straws of sleep,
> He drowned his father's magic in a dream.

A dream that drowns is a wet dream — the implication, as with the "drugged youth" of the previous poem, is sexual waste. The same implication is in the key line of the poem: "To rob me of my fluids in his heart." The manuscript version of the poem is full of specific references: "leaked their midnight seed," "the seed of dreams," "Sleep is the winding lover in my cloth." The pessimistic early draft of *I fellowed sleep* has such lines as "I fathered dreams as races from the loins" and "I fellowed sleep who drained me with a kiss." Poem Eleven in the February

1933 Notebook has perhaps the most direct statement about loss of seed:

> In wasting one drop from the heart's honey
>   cells,
> One precious drop that, for the moment, quells
> Desire's pain, eases love's itch and ills,
> There's less remains.

This sexual waste is equivalent to death. There is the boy's blunt reference in the story "A Prospect of the Sea" to "death from playing with yourself." The manuscript version of *When once the twilight locks no longer* has the lines:

> Crow on my heap, O living deaths;
> There is no horror death bequeathes
> I cannot number on this sleepy hand.

The threat Thomas sees in dreams, then, is not fanciful but physical. Sexual waste becomes the chief symbol for all the other waste of youth in the land of dreams, day dreams, night dreams, or even movies. This is why the dreams are "eunuch" and "whack their boys' limbs." They are infertile; they "groom the dark brides," but "no children break, all flavored, into light" (this line a variant in the first printing of *Our eunuch dreams*). Sexual waste, standing for all waste, is equivalent to death in life: this is the essential significance of the three dream poems.

The fight between the forces of night and day, dreams and waking action, waste of sex and proper use of sex, is part of the universal antithesis of growth and decay. The dream poems fall readily under the heading of process poems. *A process in the weather of the heart* itself uses an image that could have come from a dream poem:

> The seed that makes a forest of the loin
> Forks half its fruit; and half drops down,
> Slow in a sleeping wind.

If we wanted to be very strict about a definition of "process poem," we perhaps would have to limit it to those which utilize images (images of sexual waste, for instance, as above) to express process, and exclude those which utilize process images to express something else, the stages of growth or the harm in sexual waste, for example. This strict category would be very small, perhaps only *I see the boys of summer*, *A process in the weather of the heart*, *The force that through the green fuse drives the flower*, *Light breaks where no sun shines*, and *All all and all the dry worlds lever*. After that one draws an arbitrary line.[9] Perhaps any poem that Thomas writes in praise of mortality, even later ones such as *Poem in October*, *Fern Hill*, and *Over Sir John's hill*, has process at the core. In practice, the word "process" serves to denote those poems containing a particular kind of diction, usually accompanied by antithetical structure, giving a sense of the interplay of forces beneath the ordinary events of life.

Chapter IV

Distancing the Intimate

> *"You can put all you have to say in a single sentence and it isn't a poem. You can say God is Love, or Love is God, and have done with it—go out and play golf."*
>
> Dylan Thomas in Utah, 1952

TO EXPRESS THE IMPORTANT and intimate facts of experience without seeming to blurt them out — this is the task the poet sets himself. Thomas in his youth made several important poems from the personal, and dangerously bathetic, subject of onanism. He did so by stating sexual waste not in terms unbearably close to the subject but in remoter images such as night-mare and graveyard figures. In his marriage poems, where the secrets of the marriage bed — so to speak — are in jeopardy, much of the energy generated is in the holding back, in the forging of configurations that let out the secrets with sufficient caution, turning into fine poetry what would otherwise be mere salacious information. That these controls are esthetic rather than prudish is clear from the shamelessly sexual subject that the words do, finally, communicate. Take, for instance, the vigorous representation of sexual union in the first two stanzas of *A grief ago:*

A grief ago,
She who was who I hold, the fats and flower,
Or, water-lammed, from the scythe-sided thorn,
Hell wind and sea,
A stem cementing, wrestled up the tower,
Rose maid and male,
Or, masted venus, through the paddler's bowl
Sailed up the sun;

Who is my grief,
A chrysalis unwrinkling on the iron,
Wrenched by my fingerman, the leaden bud
Shot through the leaf,
Was who was folded on the rod the aaron
Rose cast to plague,
The horn and ball of water on the frog
Housed in the side.

Our grammar books won't let Thomas get away with "She who was who I hold." Actually few people have qualms about using "who" for "whom" where it feels natural to do so. But we might challenge the second "who" on other grounds. Is it really needed at all? Is there a significant change if we recast the lines?

A grief ago
She who I hold [did such and such].

Two things are lost by dropping the "She who was who I hold." First, the idea that the "she" now being held is a somewhat different person from the "she" who *was* being held a grief before; second, the universalizing that comes with this kind of "who," which has something of the sense of "whoever at all." The "she I hold" is a far too familiar body of bones. "She

who was who I hold" is the mysteriously estranged
loved one. We are made more remote from the particular intimate act of love, but perhaps all the closer
to the essential nature of it. The distancing is achieved
here and elsewhere by using syntax as though it were
a lock-gate, allowing meaning to come slowly through
regulated compartments. This delay in completing
the sense is important in dealing with intimate things;
it avoids the danger of flippancy. Moreover, to dis-
turb customary syntax is to affect normal space and
time relationships. *A grief ago* takes place all within
the few moments after sexual union, but by means
of the syntax we are flashed back to genesis and
forward to the day of judgment; the history of the
world is concentrated into the moment.

Thomas' abnormal syntax may occasionally be
confusing; but it is rare that grammatical requirements
are not rigorously met. The first stanza of *A grief ago*
is a good test case. If we italicize the three main
verbs, the actions of the subject "she," and enclose
in brackets appositional descriptive material (adverbs
being put into parentheses), the stanza becomes:

> (A grief ago,)
> She [who was who I hold,] [the fats and
>   flower,]
> [Or, water-lammed, (from the scythe-sided
>   thorn,)
> Hell wind and sea,]
> [A stem cementing,] *wrestled* (up the tower),
> *Rose* [maid and male],
> Or [, masted venus,] (through the paddler's
>   bowl)
> *Sailed* (up the sun).

The stanza is clearly a "she did something" sentence. That "something" is one action; but Thomas uses syntax that will allow for three very active verbs, each with graphic adverbial adjuncts, while adding several appositional descriptions of the "she," all this with correct, though difficult, grammar.

Literary craftsmanship has traditionally met the challenge of blank paper by such devices of amplification and compression. *A Refusal to Mourn the Death, by Fire, of a Child in London* is in the same tradition as, though a good deal more serious than, Chaucer's *occupatio*, the rhetorical technique of confessing it to be beyond his skill to describe what he then goes on to describe. The "I am dumb to tell" of *The force that through the green fuse drives the flower* is the same device of volubly protesting a lack of words. And there are many other techniques. The rhetorical question, which goes at least part of the way to answering itself, is common in Thomas:

> What shall it tell me if a timeless insect
> Says the world wears away?
> >   (*Here in this spring*).

It structures the first two stanzas of *How shall my animal* and the opening lines of *Vision and Prayer*. Thomas has messengers within his poems. "I tell her this" in *A grief ago* is a good example. Quaintly, in *A Winter's Tale*, the tale itself is brought into the poem like a boat, "pale breath of cattle at the stealthy sail." *Poem in October* opens with the morning beckoning the poet with its harbor noises. In *Over Sir John's hill* the poet reads psalms in "the leaves of the water" and hears "death" in a shell. The first half of the *Ballad of the Long-legged Bait* is mainly made up of running commentary from a number of incidental personae such as "the dwindling ships" and "the laughing fish." One happy form of amplification is to express the negative of what *doesn't* happen in order to communicate what *does:*

> . . . the lover's rub
> That wipes away not crow's-foot nor the lock
> Of sick old manhood on the fallen jaws
> > (*If I were tickled by the rub of love*);

or to pretend ignorance of which of two possibilities pertains, where both (or neither, as in the case of dreams and movies in *Our eunuch dreams*) apply:

> I know not whether
> Adam or Eve, the adorned holy bullock
> Or the white ewe lamb
> Or the chosen virgin
> Laid in her snow
> On the altar of London,
> Was the first to die
> > (*Ceremony After a Fire Raid*).

An extreme example of this use of the rhetorical negative is in the Prayer part of *Vision and Prayer*, where the poet prays in the name of the wrong people:

> In the name of the lost who glory in
> The swinish plains of carrion
>
> .   .   .   .
>
> In the name of the wanton
> Lost on the unchristened mountain
>
> .   .   .   .

O in the name
Of no one
Now or

No
One to
Be . . .

But he is praying, in their unholy or nonexistent
names, for the *opposite* of what he wants. He prays

That he [Christ] let the dead lie though they moan
For his briared hands to hoist them
To the shrine of his world's wound

. . . . . .

May the crimson
Sun spin a grave grey
And the color of clay
Stream upon his martyrdom.

All this could have been done much more easily with
a single positive statement; but two wrongs make a
right — and also a poem.

The choice of metaphor, as well as the syntac-
tical arrangement, is an important factor in distancing.
The man in the street is often an expert at handling
sexual matters with images that utilize metaphoric
wordplay. Few would be unwilling to concede
Thomas supremacy in this area, however. See him
at work in the first stanza of *A grief ago*, where the
girl's motions are the focus of attention. Cementing
a stem, she wrestles up the tower; rises maid and
male; as a masted venus, she sails up the sun through
the paddler's bowl. These are images for the welcom-
ing of penetration, a highly erotic subject; but
Thomas has managed to find words that communicate

the event without eroticism. "Masted venus" — why doesn't this image, a most dynamic way of saying that the female is completely possessed ("masted") by the male, strike us as prurient? One reason is the sharpness of the wording, the opposite of slyness. Further, the image, as well as being sexually symbolic, has to take its place in the literal image-narrative. The venus is masted *like a boat* and, in the next line, *sails*. The sailing image is remote from any pictorial representation of joined parts of the body.

Another description of complete penetration, in *The tombstone told when she died*, is a contrast:

> I died before bedtime came
> But my womb was bellowing
> And I felt with my bare fall
> A blazing red harsh head tear up
> And the dear floods of his hair.

Thomas himself was troubled by this warmer, closer imagery:

> The word "dear" fits in, I think, with "though her eyes smiled," which comes earlier. I wanted the girl's *terrible* reaction to orgastic [sic] death to be suddenly altered into a kind of despairing love. As I see it now, it strikes me as very moving, but it may be too much of a shock, a bathetic shock perhaps.[1]

Yes, the passage *is* moving and vivid (the "hair" is pubic hair), which is just what the imagery of *A grief ago* isn't. To be moved one must be struck by a familiar chord. Perhaps the most immediately moving lines in *A grief ago* are:

Tugged through the days
Her ropes of heritage.

They draw on a fairly conventional image of struggle
and oppression. But in these lines — and those from
The tombstone told when she died — Thomas is least
himself. He is most himself when he has forced us
to take a new view of something (a "masted venus"
for instance) by putting us at a distance from the
intimate.

[2]

Freud discovered that the unconscious or sleeping mind is a great coiner of euphemistic metaphors,
and that the coinage shows certain consistencies. To
know about the specific figures that the unconscious
mind repeatedly uses as metaphors should, on the
face of it, be useful in studying poetry. After all,
poetry is at one stage or another a heeding of the
sights and sounds from the muse in the unconscious.
But, strictly speaking, Freudian symbols arise from
the need of our minds "to give a *disguised* representation to their latent thoughts."[2] Freud is really dealing with what happens when the mind works against
itself. Only when we find an author *unwittingly* producing symbols we recognize as Freudian can we
apply Freud's theory — though one might challenge
the value of reading into a work levels of meaning
of which the author was not himself aware. Thomas
was very clear on this point. His answer to the *New
Verse* question on Freudian influence shows him to
be well aware of the significance of repression and

actively interested in combatting it. He wanted to go further than Freud:

> Poetry must drag further into the clean nakedness of light more even of the hidden causes than Freud could realize.[3]

Thus the applicability of Freud to Thomas seems severely limited. The symbolism behind which a repressed mind hides itself should be approached differently from the symbolism by means of which the poet consciously desires to reveal.

At the same time, the well-known Freudian symbols constitute a shared sexual language. Everything today is either concave or convex. Such a word as "crocodile" (used twice by Thomas) can gain a simple denotative meaning from being in the Freudian bestiary. Thomas must have known he was being Freudian in certain places — the dream sequences at the beginning of *Under Milk Wood*, for instance. Another case, perhaps, is in *Into her Lying Down Head*. A room generally represents a woman, and the snake is the most important symbol of the male member.[4] So we can decode the sexual event behind the words:

> There where a numberless tongue
> Wound their room with a male moan,
> His faith around her flew undone
> And darkness hung the walls with baskets of
> snakes.

As Thomas puts it: "Man is denying his partner man or woman and whores with the whole night."[5] The question, however, is whether or not we really need recourse to Freud. The associational logic that our dreaming mind is said to exhibit in its symbol-making is equally available to our waking mind. If the sleeping mind "deceives" itself with a dream of Aaron's rod, for instance, the poet should be able to use the same analogizing process in order to communicate deliberately the sexual significance. We simply do not need Freud to tell us that scythe, thorn, stem, tower, mast, paddle, and sun are male symbols, and fats, flower, and bowl are female; nor to divulge the secret of the water imagery in the mythology of *A grief ago:* "The people's sea drives on her"; "The dens of shape / Shape all her whelps with the long voice of water"; "Let her inhale her dead, through seed and solid / Draw in their seas." Water and the sea are naturally associated with conception and birth; the physical processes involve fluids at every stage, seminal to amniotic. And one does not feel especially relieved to find this association confirmed by Freud. What Freud contributes to an understanding of sexual imagery is just what we can now (post-Freudians that we are) most take for granted, i.e. that sexual matters will generally be imaged by some physically similar counterpart. One tussles with the intricacy of Thomas' imagery in somewhat the same manner as Freud tackled dreams, but trusting that the poet's creating, censoring, and selecting mind has a responsibility and skill that the dreaming mind does not; in short, that the distancing is esthetic rather than psychotic, conscious rather than the result of repression in the unconscious.

Let us see, then, with or without Freud, what we can make of perhaps the most obscure and involved sexual imagery in *A grief ago:*

[She] Was who was folded on the rod the aaron
Rose cast to plague,
The horn and ball of water on the frog
Housed in the side.

The context indicates that the girl is folded on
(wrapped around) a male rod. This rod is described
as the one which "the aaron rose cast to plague." In
the Biblical story, "Aaron stretched out his hand with
his rod, and smote the dust of the earth, and it became
lice." For the second applicable meaning of "plague"
we turn back to *From love's first fever to her plague*
where the word means "production of offspring."
Plague breeds, and children are a pestilence. So that
when the "aaron rose" (i.e. herself acting like Aaron)
casts the rod to plague, she can be said to be creating
children by means of it, "cast" recalling the fishing
image for sexual reproduction in *Ballad of the Long-
legged Bait*. The masculinity of "aaron" is softened
by an echo of the feminine "sharon rose." "Rose"
itself is a common symbol for the female. No one
can doubt what is going on when we have rod and
rose together. But no more than in previous instances
is the imagery erotic. The complexity makes its own
demands on our attention, and thus keeps us at a
distance from the sexual event.

"Horn and ball of water on the frog" is perhaps
even more difficult. Grammar indicates that the phrase
is equivalent to the "rod" above. "Horn," at least,
has well-established phallic connotations. "Ball" added
to "horn" is, one presumes, completing a stylized representation. "Of water" makes a connection with
"water-lammed" in the first stanza and the other
water imagery generally symbolic of insemination and

gestation. The horn and ball of water are "housed in the side" — the Miltonic sense of "side" as the womb. "On the frog" is not only grotesque but unclear. "Frog" probably has its root meaning of "jump." Brought into the poem because of the Egyptian plague of frogs — another of Thomas' superficial associations — the image evokes the sufficiently suggestive physical action, leap-frog. The wording "on the frog" denotes a continuous action, like "on the hop" or "on the make." One has no need to investigate what the phrase might mean to a patient of Freud's, but rather what possible ways there are of playing on the normal meaning of "frog" and "leap-frog." One enters Thomas' sexual imagery, like his other imagery, through the dictionary meanings and the verbal turns he seems likely to be making.

Provided there is an essential connectedness between the thing and the distancing image, the remoter the image the more esthetically effective it is. Hence the telling use of death imagery for sexual matters. Love and death are, paradoxically, both far apart and very close. This paradox, which gives the title of *A grief ago* its significance, is at the core of the conception stanzas of the poem:

> And she who lies,
> Like exodus a chapter from the garden,
> Brand of the lily's anger on her ring,
> Tugged through the days
> Her ropes of heritage, the wars of pardon,
> On field and sand
> The twelve triangles of the cherub wind
> Engraving going.

Who then is she,
She holding me? The people's sea drives on her,
Drives out the father from the caesared camp;
The dens of shape
Shape all her whelps with the long voice of
    water,
That she I have,
The country-handed grave boxed into love,
Rise before dark.

The night is near,
A nitric shape that leaps her, time and acid;
I tell her this: before the suncock cast
Her bone to fire,
Let her inhale her dead, through seed and solid
Draw in their seas,
So cross her hand with their grave gipsy eyes,
And close her fist.

Behind the wit of "And she who lies,/Like exodus a chapter from the garden," which uses Old Testament imagery to denote the resting of the withdrawn couple, is the serious identification of the girl with Eve and of the sexual act with the first sin against purity in Eden. God's command to go out and multiply was coincident with His imposing the penalty of mortality. It is as though death forces one to love. Thomas gives us the image of the grave "boxing" the girl into love. The grave has "countries" for hands, countries a symbol of national and personal history and endurance — as in the lines:

[She] Tugged through the days
Her ropes of heritage, the wars of pardon,
On field and sand

> The twelve triangles of the cherub wind
> Engraving going.

The tug-of-war image represents the burden that the
Fall has imposed. The wind is the agent of death,
not only wearing the girl down, but engraving,
bringing her to her grave. Death is the lover who
leaps her — and then we have the lover as the herald
of doomsday and also, with the apocalyptic "suncock"
and its connotations of male potency, of birth. There
is a long literary tradition for lovers dying in sex,
but Thomas' is a far more serious use of the conceit
than probably any since the seventeenth century.
The dead hover over the conception; they are in a
mystical way the ingredients of life: "Let her inhale
her dead."

[3]

Thomas often expresses the sexual in religious
terms. With characteristic frankness and sacrilegious-
ness — frank and sacrilegious because the cross, as
something that has to be borne, cannot escape phallic
connotations in this poem — the "old ram rod" of
Lament sighs:

> When I was a man you could call a man
> And the black cross of the holy house.

Thomas can say with truth, "I know the legend / Of
Adam and Eve is never for a second / Silent in my
service" (*Ceremony After a Fire Raid*). In a sense,
the religious merely serves for esthetic purposes. The
range of basically non-sacred religious imagery runs
from the casual

And the sabbath rang slowly
In the pebbles of the holy streams
                    (*Fern Hill*)

to the emphatic

No. Not for Christ's dazzling bed
        ('*If my head hurt a hair's foot*').

At times Christ is used as a simile:

The young stars told me,
Hurling into beginning like Christ the child
                    (*Unluckily for a Death*).

But then we have the reverse situation. Christ appears as Himself in some poems, and metaphors are then found for Him. And just as Christ is used rather cavalierly in figures of speech, so are rather cavalier figures of speech found for Christ. There is sometimes real doubt whether Christ is being praised or defamed. In the Buffalo notebooks, an undated epigram reads, in part:

If God is praised in poem one
Show no surprise when in the next
I worship wood or sun or none.

One of Thomas' first published poems, in *Adelphi* (September 1933), has the same duality:

No man believes who cries not, God is not,

        . . . .

Believe and be saved. No man believes
Who curses not what makes and saves.

        . . . .

> And this is true, no man can live
> Who does not bury God in a deep grave
> And then raise up the skeleton again.

The same scorn seems to appear in such poems as *Incarnate devil* and *Shall gods be said to thump the clouds* to say nothing of more juvenile poems left in manuscript. But *Before I knocked* is a different matter; it is a harsh, sincere reaction to the idea of Christ's mortality:

> You who bow down at cross and altar,
> Remember me and pity Him
> Who took my flesh and bone for armour
> And doublecrossed my mother's womb.

This harshness, and the "Jack of Christ" in other poems, is a deliberate distancing device, whose effect lies in the commitment to a deity that one dares disparage. Thomas talked of his father's atheism, an atheism which

> had nothing to do with whether there was a god or not, but was a violent and personal dislike for God. He would glare out of the window and growl: "It's raining, blast Him!" or, "The sun is shining — Lord, what foolishness!"[6]

Thomas' own attitude to Christ is probably closer to his father's than to that of Hopkins or Francis Thompson, say. Even in his most devotional poem, *Vision and Prayer*, Thomas has achieved distancing (paradoxically) by getting so close to the birth of Christ that it ceases to be a sentimental nativity and becomes the birth of the poet's own child in the next room.

To avoid identifying the chief character, certainly one way of distancing, is one of the several means used in Thomas' other main Christian document, the sonnet sequence *Altarwise by owl-light*. In the first sonnet he is "the gentleman," and "that gentleman of wounds" (which helps); but he is other things as well:

> Altarwise by owl-light in the half-way house
> The gentleman lay graveward with his furies;
> Abaddon in the hangnail cracked from Adam,
> And, from his fork, a dog among the fairies,
> The atlas-eater with a jaw for news,
> Bit out the mandrake with to-morrow's scream.
> Then, penny-eyed, that gentleman of wounds,
> Old cock from nowheres and the heaven's egg,
> With bones unbuttoned to the half-way winds,
> Hatched from the windy salvage on one leg,
> Scraped at my cradle in a walking word
> That night of time under the Christward shelter:
> I am the long world's gentleman, he said,
> And share my bed with Capricorn and Cancer.

We have previously glanced at the "atlas-eater" lines in taking up Thomas' complaint that Edith Sitwell didn't read them literally. Thomas gave the "literal" reading:

> a world-devouring ghost creature bit out the horror of to-morrow from a gentleman's loins.[7]

In other words, this is a form of castration. One thinks immediately of sonnet VIII:

> I by the tree of thieves, all glory's sawbones,
> Unsex the skeleton this mountain minute.

Again, the religious is expressed in sexual terms, the violence of the crucifixion being like a castration, the sacrifice a self-castration. Gods of other cultures have performed this act; but the whole problem is made more difficult in sonnet I by the castration's being performed by a strange creature described first as a dog and then an atlas-eater. And Thomas doesn't clarify too much in his further "literal" interpretation of the lines. There is no hint of the Christian key:

> A "jaw for news" is an obvious variation of a "nose for news", and means that the mouth of the creature can taste already the horror that has not yet come, or can sense its coming, can thrust its tongue into the news that has not yet been made, can savour the enormity of the progeny before the seed stirs, can realise the crumbling of dead flesh before the opening of the womb that delivers that flesh to to-morrow. What is this creature? It's the dog among the fairies, the rip and cur among the myths, the snapper at demons, the scarer of ghosts, the wizard's heel-chaser.[8]

Trying to make the creature seem a literal atlas-eater with a jaw for news, he keeps re-phrasing the image. He tries to find synonyms for the dog among the fairies. But, imagination having got the better of analysis, he is in effect writing a continuation of the poem. We are left to do the analyzing. The creature that bites out the mandrake is, in its simplest terms, biting out a symbol of mortality; the creature senses the "crumbling of dead flesh" and bites it out. The event just before this in the poem is syntactically an exact parallel: "Abaddon in the hangnail" cracks off from Adam.[9] "Adam" is Christ the Man, the second Adam, in this crucifixion scene. "Abaddon in the hangnail" is the devil, the devil in the flesh, another symbol for sin and mortality. The event is the Redemption. Man is being released from sin and death through the physical violence done to Christ's body. Who performs this physical violence? In the first image, the Abaddon cracks off without an agent being present. In the castration image proper, the agent is the "atlas-eater," whom Thomas describes as a "world-devouring ghost creature." Let us take him up on that word *ghost*, and postulate the Holy Ghost, who certainly is a "wizard's heel-chaser" (i.e. "a dog among the fairies") in the sense brought out in Milton's "Nativity Ode," one of Thomas' favorite poems, the pagan gods fleeing before Him. It is perhaps better not to stick to the conventional Trinity. Rather let us put it that the spiritual element in the Christ figure is working the miracle of Redemption on the physical Christ, the "sawbones" (doctor, who heals, saves) aspect of Christ operating on the "skeleton" Christ, as sonnet VIII has it. After all, it is none other than Christ himself who gave himself up to torture and death. This is a one-man drama, which Thomas splits into multiple roles.

It is basic to Thomas' idiom that a person should divide and walk on two levels, and see himself walking there. The Godhead does this in *Before I knocked:*

I, born of flesh and ghost, was neither
A ghost nor man, but mortal ghost.
And I was struck down by death's feather.
I was mortal to the last

> Long breath that carried to my father
> The message of his dying christ.

The ordinary individual can be a trinity in himself:

> My hero bares my side and sees his heart
> Tread, like a naked Venus,
> The beach of flesh, and wind her bloodred plait
>   (*My hero bares his nerves*);

> I sent my creature scouting on the globe,
> That globe itself of hair and bone
> That, sewn to me by nerve and brain,
> Had stringed my flask of matter to his rib
>   (*When once the twilight locks no longer*).

We have to be sure of this ingrained notion of split-identity in Thomas, because it is the only reasonable key to the first sonnet.[10] For Christ is not only on the Cross (and, as we have seen, the Redemption involves more than one aspect of His personality), but He is also the Christ child in the cradle:

> [The gentleman of wounds]
> Scraped at my cradle in a walking word
> That night of time under the Christward shelter.

The "Christward shelter" gives us the nativity scene; there is no point in trying to imagine the poet in a Swansea cradle. The use of "my" is just another example of the "me-Him" split that we come across so often in Thomas. Here Christ just off the Cross comes to visit the newly-born Christ. The Nativity is put against the backdrop of Calvary. It is as though the Babe were being told the significance of His incarnation "in a walking word" by the Christ who has just "Hatched from the windy salvage on one leg." "Hatched" is the key word in the sonnet. It refers to the crucifixion: "on one leg" is a grotesquely simple way of speaking of the upright of the Cross, and "the windy salvage" is this world of mortality, a "salvage" because it is the thing saved by Christ. Though used to indicate death, "hatched" has at the same time all the connotations of birth, birth into everlasting life, Christ's second nativity. Thomas' sonnet sequence on the significance of Christ, then, begins appropriately with the Nativity as the subject of the first sonnet — but the Nativity approached so obliquely that we have to shed all conventional sentiments by the time we arrive at it. This is the final aim of distancing: not to obscure, but to prevent us from rushing in with the hackneyed, with our own notions rather than the poet's.

Chapter V

Last Poems

*"I consider that it is the chief duty
of the interpreter to begin analyses
and to leave them unfinished."*

C. S. Lewis, *Allegory of Love*

WE HAVE ATTEMPTED TO SEE what lies behind the obscurity of Thomas' early poetry; with the last poems we have to ask what lies behind their comparative clarity. The "Note" to the *Collected Poems*, dated November 1952, seems especially applicable to the later poems of the volume: they were written "for the love of Man and in praise of God." But behind that solemnity one can hear the poet's alternative phrasing to John Malcolm Brinnin in July 1951: "poems in praise of God's world by a man who doesn't believe in God."[1] The answer to the riddle posed by these statements is perhaps best sought in the poems themselves, for instance in *Over Sir John's hill* where universal mortality is symbolized in the actual scene from the poet's window overlooking the estuary of the Taf and Towy at Laugharne, South Wales. God is mentioned twice in the poem; we seek the significance of these two allusions:

Over Sir John's hill,
The hawk on fire hangs still;

In a hoisted cloud, at drop of dusk, he pulls to
    his claws
And gallows, up the rays of his eyes the small
    birds of the bay
And the shrill child's play
Wars
Of the sparrows and such who swansing, dusk,
    in wrangling hedges.
And blithely they squawk
To fiery tyburn over the wrestle of elms until
The flash the noosed hawk
Crashes, and slowly the fishing holy stalking
    heron
In the river Towy below bows his tilted
    headstone.

Flash, and the plumes crack,
And a black cap of jack-
Daws Sir John's just hill dons, and again the
    gulled birds hare
To the hawk on fire, the halter height, over
    Towy's fins,
In a whack of wind.
There
Where the elegiac fisherbird stabs and paddles
In the pebbly dab-filled
Shallow and sedge, and 'dilly dilly,' calls the loft
    hawk,
'Come and be killed,'
I open the leaves of the water at a passage
Of psalms and shadows among the pincered
    sandcrabs prancing

And read, in a shell,
Death clear as a buoy's bell:

All praise of the hawk on fire in hawk-eyed dusk
    be sung,
When his viperish fuse hangs looped with flames
    under the brand
Wing, and blest shall
Young
Green chickens of the bay and bushes cluck,
    'dilly dilly,
Come let us die.'
We grieve as the blithe birds, never again, leave
    shingle and elm,
The heron and I,
I young Aesop fabling to the near night by the
    dingle
Of eels, saint heron hymning in the shell-hung
    distant

Crystal harbour vale
Where the sea cobbles sail,
And wharves of water where the walls dance
    and the white cranes stilt.
It is the heron and I, under judging Sir John's
    elmed
Hill, tell-tale the knelled
Guilt
Of the led-astray birds whom God, for their
    breast of whistles,
Have mercy on,
God in his whirlwind silence save, who marks
    the sparrows hail,
For their souls' song.
Now the heron grieves in the weeded verge.
    Through windows
Of dusk and water I see the tilting whispering

Heron, mirrored, go,
As the snapt feathers snow,
Fishing in the tear of the Towy. Only a hoot owl
Hollows, a grassblade blown in cupped hands,
    in the looted elms
And no green cocks or hens
Shout
Now on Sir John's hill. The heron, ankling the
    scaly
Lowlands of the waves,
Makes all the music; and I who hear the tune of
    the slow
Wear-willow river, grave,
Before the lunge of the night, the notes on this
    time-shaken
Stone for the sake of the souls of the slain birds
    sailing.

Do sparrows have souls? In what theological
sense can they possibly be saved? Or, to recast the
question in keeping with the parable nature of the
poem, do human beings (with their "shrill, child's-
play wars") have immortal souls whose destiny depends on God's mercy being evoked by prayer? The
same kind of question attends the basic courtroom
metaphor in the poem. As often before, Thomas is
acting out a common expression: "We are all condemned to die." In the traditional religious sense we
are *condemned* by Adam's original sin, and are per-
sonally *saved* by the redemption of Christ. The use
of "save," "blest," "mercy," etc. in the poem suggests
the traditional approach; but the poem doesn't really
go beyond the mere suggestion. The word "guilt" is
used, but without seriously indicating in what sense
the small birds (or we unknown soldiers) are guilty.

Although Sir John's hill puts on the black cap for our death sentence, there is no real judgment as there is no real crime. Where a little sermonizing of the scene might be expected in the poem, one looks in vain. The hawk-executioner, especially, might have been given moral import; but the poet's intention seems to have been quite the opposite.

It is worth-while looking closely at the language used to describe the hawk, and this is one case where there is little doubt as to the kind of decision that produced the particular wording. Harvard College Library has the working papers for this poem, and although they are extensive and cumbersome (forty-seven sheets for the single poem), we can with a high degree of accuracy follow the poet from the first conception to the completed poem. Some phrases are worked and reworked up to forty-one times. We are given an opportunity to see exactly what kind of pains Thomas took. Pertinent to our concern with the personality, if any, of the hawk is the phrase "halter height" in the second stanza of the poem:

> . . . and again the gulled birds hare
> To the hawk on fire, the halter height, over
>   Towy's fins.

As we might expect, the words are descriptive and symbolic at the same time. The hawk catches the last rays of the sun and is "on fire" — this is apt description. But it is also symbolic, connected to the doomsday-explosion symbolism running through the poem, by which the hawk is viewed as a gunpowder fuse ready to go off. Thus, the hawk is as much a metaphor for the symbolic fire as the fire is a metaphoric way of describing the hawk. The poet's efforts in the work sheets are directed toward finding the diction that will successfully act this double role, symbolic description and descriptive symbolism.

The "hawk on fire" in the passage above began, it seems, quite simply as the "high hawk." What appears to be the next draft incorporates both the gallows and the gunpowder images in "the hempen firing hawk," a foreshadowing of the final phrase, "the hawk on fire, the halter height." The work sheets often show that first thoughts are the best, but the poet proves it to himself by trying out alternatives. In subsequent rewritings of this part of the poem we find him substituting different phrases while simply recopying the adjacent lines. He introduces a brutal image of slaughter: "the skinning hawk." Then, as though to soften somewhat the picture of tearing flesh, the hawk is abstracted to one aspect of itself, its height above the bay. Thus we have "the skinning height" that the small birds hare to. But "skinning" is subsequently replaced by a reversion to the gallows theme with "the hanging height." Soon "hanging," not quite right, is intensified to "lynching." "The lynching height" appears several times in the drafts while the poet adjusts such phrases as "over the river Towy finned," neatened to "over Towy's fins." Then there is one particular three square inches of a page in which Thomas lists further possibilities—"dusky height," "hempen height," and "hempen caudle height." "Caudle," a sweet drink, is appropriate to the gaiety with which the little victims fly up to their death. But, further, "hempen caudle" has been used by Shakespeare to mean "a hanging," and no doubt Thomas was thinking of following suit.[2] But neither this nor any of the others seems to have been as satisfactory as "lynching height," which is used as a stand-by until finally crossed out in favor of "halter height" near the end of the work on the poem.

"Halter height" is not the choice that might have appealed to some poets. It is more cold and bloodless than "skinning" and "lynching," for instance. The only explanation for Thomas' passing over these more violent words is that their connotations must have been undesirable. They both imply vindictiveness; whereas "halter" does not. The work sheets show Thomas deliberately finding a neutral adjective for his killer-hawk. He does not want death to appear hateful. As for "hempen," which is neutral enough, it gives perhaps an unwanted notion of texture; the hawk is not a sack but a noose. There was possibly nothing wrong with "hanging height" except commonplaceness. "Halter" says the same thing as "hanging" but more interestingly. "Halter" is also the harness for a driven animal. Besides the point that death is amoral and unjudging, Thomas seems to want to say that mortality is a burden taken on by all. Like the sea of *A Refusal to Mourn the Death, by Fire, of a Child in London*, we are all "tumbling in harness"; and the "halter" here signifies the final pull of that harness.

Death is not just (or unjust), Sir John's hill is not judging, the birds are not guilty, the heron is not holy, and God is not, in any meaningful sense, merciful. What, then, are we to think of a poem in which such adjectives are applied to such individuals?

Perhaps we should bear in mind, to begin with, that the common expression "condemned to die" does not, when one thinks about it, really mean condemned, *punished* by death. It is just a way of saying "shall or will die" — simple futurity. But there is a rightness about "condemned"; it corresponds to the feeling of grievance against death. The word is not irresponsible; neither, I think, is Thomas. The poem may be expressing only the *fact* of death, and such words as "guilt" may be empty of intellectual content; but a form of meaning is communicated to the emotions, the reader's compassion is guided. One usually frowns on poetry that has vague emotional wording without precise denotation. Such a dismissal would not, I think, meet the case here. Thomas should be given credit for expressing truly the chief tenet of the non-religious: that the intellect cannot handle the fact of death, and that it is sternness, rebellion, hatred, self-pity, compassion — some naked emotion — with which we are left to face the situation. From among these emotions it is Thomas' inclination to choose compassion and to use the words, new or old, which will succeed in expressing it for him.

We get a closer look at the God of *Over Sir John's hill* in a prose note about a projected long poem to be entitled *In Country Heaven*, of which that poem along with *In country sleep* and *In the white giant's thigh* would form separate parts. The frame for the pieces is the scene in heaven when God hears of the end of the world:

> The godhead, the author, the milky-way farmer, the first cause, architect, lamplighter, quintessence, the beginning Word, the an-

thropomorphic bowler-out and black-baller,
the stuff of all men, scapegoat, martyr,
maker, woe-bearer He, on top of a hill in
Heaven, weeps whenever, outside that state
of being called his country, one of his worlds
drops dead, vanishes screaming, shrivels, ex-
plodes, murders itself. And, when he weeps,
Light and His tears glide down together,
hand in hand. So, at the beginning of the
projected poem, he weeps, and Country
Heaven is suddenly dark. Bushes and owls
blow out like candles. And the countrymen
of heaven crouch all together under the
hedges and, among themselves in the tear-
salt darkness, surmise which world, which
star, which of their late, turning homes, in
the skies has gone for ever. And this time,
spreads the heavenly hedgerow rumour, it
is the Earth. The Earth has killed itself. It is
black, petrified, wizened, poisoned, burst;
insanity has blown it rotten; and no creatures at all, joyful, despairing, cruel, kind,
dumb, afire, loving, dull, shortly and brut-
ishly hunt their days down like enemies on
that corrupted face. And, one by one, these
heavenly hedgerow-men, who once were of
the Earth, call one another, through the long
night, Light and His tears falling, what they
remember, what they sense in the submerged
wilderness and on the exposed hairsbreadth
of the mind, what they feel trembling on the
nerves of a nerve, what they know in their
Edenic hearts, of that self-called place. They
remember places, fears, loves, exultation,

misery, animal joy, ignorance and mysteries, all *we* know and do not know.

The poem is made of these tellings. And the poem becomes, at last, an affirmation of the beautiful and terrible worth of the Earth. It grows into a praise of what is and what could be on this lump in the skies. It is a poem about happiness.[3]

Dylan Thomas, supposedly the lyric poet, the singer of the self, is in these last poems responding perhaps as fully as any writer of our time to the basic problem facing mankind in the atomic age, the problem of total annihilation. Furthermore, his response is particularly suited to what C. S. Lewis would call our post-Christian era or what Albert Camus would call the age of absurdity. For Thomas' God, both in the prose account and in the poems, is not a religious entity at all in the normal sense of a presiding Being whose presence controls or at least justifies our existence. Thomas' God does nothing to alleviate the absurdity of the position of rational man in an irrational universe; Thomas' God does nothing to explain death in terms of higher values. As the eternal sympathetic spectator, He simply weeps, offering none of the usual consolations. It is the Last Day of Non-Judgment:

> And all your deeds and words,
> Each truth, each lie,
> Die in unjudging love
> (*This side of the Truth*).

One can see why Thomas said he didn't "believe in God" — not the usual God, anyway. His own God has perhaps only one function: to make death less fearful. Or, looked at the other way round, that miraculous force which — not for any arguable reason but nevertheless effectively — makes death less fearful, he calls God.

Some of the early poems saw death as a threat, a "running grave." In the first London days it was understood that the poet would die within a few years.[4] There is reason to believe that he had had vague intimations from a doctor. But one detects no real sense of imminent death until the last poems, in which Thomas seems to gauge his life-span exactly. *Poem on his Birthday* (his thirty-fifth) acknowledges the approaching death (four years later). Yet he meets it with an increased momentum of life:

> . . . the closer I move
> To death, one man through his sundered hulks,
> The louder the sun blooms
> And the tusked, ramshackling sea exults;
> And every wave of the way
> And gale I tackle, the whole world then,
> With more triumphant faith
> Than ever was since the world was said,
> Spins its morning of praise.

And the *Author's Prologue* (1952), with which he sealed his life's work, is written

> For you to know
> How I, a spinning man,
> Glory also this star, bird
> Roared, sea born, man torn, blood blest.
> Hark: I trumpet the place,
> From fish to jumping hill! Look:
> I build my bellowing ark

> To the best of my love
> As the flood begins.

It need not, therefore, be a mystery why the hawk is praised in *Over Sir John's hill*:

> All praise of the hawk on fire in hawk-eyed
> dusk be sung.

His call is seductive: "Dilly dilly, come and be killed." And it is blithely answered: "Dilly dilly, come let us die." This poem about death is a celebration; "it is a poem about happiness." The Thief in *In country sleep*, like the hawk, is not really an enemy. He is "sly," as the conceit demands; but he is also "sure." The dominant mood of the poem is assurance. Thomas' message to his sleeping child is that the Thief will not leave her forsaken. To paraphrase a very complicated sentence: she has a faith that each night Death comes to dispel her fear that he will leave her to grieve he will not come. Sleep is a small death, and confirms each night death's presence in the world.

> My dear this night he comes and night without
> end my dear
>   Since you were born:
> And you shall wake, from country sleep, this
> dawn and each first dawn,
> Your faith as deathless as the outcry of the ruled
> sun.

The sun, no less than mere mortals, is "ruled" (or "chained," as it was in a draft). One's sustaining faith is two-edged: life is given security by being bounded by death.

Death can be personified and symbolized; pathos

is a ready emotion. But a fulness of life cannot successfully be shown as a person or a symbol. It has
to be described in its particulars so that every word
upholds the assertion of value with an intrinsic
buoyancy. "Buoyancy" is hardly definable; much
depends upon poetic effects whose qualities — though
one can talk bluntly about alliteration and rhyme —
fortunately defy analysis. Poetic effects should not
demand admiration, but should keep us admiring un-
awares. The exuberant life recalled by the dead
women of *In the white giant's thigh* is so detailed and
passionate that one hardly notices that the poem is
written in quatrains; the "daughters of darkness flame
like Fawkes fires still," but their longing for children
(a *symbol* of affirmative life, if you will) is so keen
that one doesn't remark how very alliterative they
are. In this example from stanza two of *Over Sir
John's hill:*

> There
> Where the elegiac fisherbird stabs and paddles
> In the pebbly dab-filled
> Shallow and sedge . . . ,

one can feel that the sound of "there where" goes
very well with the idea called for by "elegiac," and
that the verse ensures the shallow is sufficiently filled
with dabs. One does not count consonants to prove
how many fish. Suffice it to say that the words flick
one's attention from object to action to object in a
real, active world. We might, however, be permitted
one question: Is "sedge" added to "shallow" for
more reason than the sound effect? It introduces a
useful but inconsequential detail — "sedge" is marshy

grass. But this doesn't prevent our repeating: Is this word alliteration-determined? Does anything else help it deserve its place?

The question can be answered satisfactorily when we go further into the meaning of "sedge" — and with the aid of the Harvard work sheets. Funk and Wagnall's Dictionary gives a second meaning: "A flock of herons or similar birds." The word has the same meaning as "siege" as listed in the *OED:* "The station of a heron on the watch for prey." It is then technically correct for Thomas to have his fisherbird in a "sedge," and it is all to the good to have this further note added to the theme of universal predatoriness. Thomas' intention is evident in the work sheets. A circled note reads: "Sedge is a lot of herons." Near it is the phrase, "a sedge of heron stilts." The poet did not use this ready-made combination. Elsewhere, however, he was having trouble finding a meaningful word to fit a much-favored sound pattern. Throughout the drafts we find the variants: "shallow and shadow," "shallow and shade," "shallow and stones," "shallow and shelves." Thomas' discovery that "sedge" is loaded with two meanings suitable for his context, as well as having the right sound, made "shallow and sedge" the natural end to the search. This phrase, unlike "the hawk on fire, the halter height," for instance, may not add too much to the serious symbolic thread of the poem; but the very vitality of such descriptive language deepens the significance of a song in praise of mortality, which can be said to succeed in so far as the diction vies with life itself in being active and many-sided.

It seems beside the point to add that Dylan

Thomas died young, that he died amidst hullabaloo in New York City. His last work, *Under Milk Wood*, was a great comedy; his last words were a humorous play on "roses" and "Rose's" (lime juice);[5] and, most of all, his last poems give a sense of what it is to live well and die well, so that even an unillusioned age, "a lump in the skies," might feel that, in some inexplicable way, life is a blessing and death is a *good* night.

Abbreviations

Thomas' works:

18P	*18 Poems* (London: The Sunday Referee and the Parton Bookshop, 1934)
25P	*Twenty-five Poems* (London: J. M. Dent & Sons, 1936)
ML	*The Map of Love* (London: J. M. Dent & Sons, 1939)
Portrait	*Portrait of the Artist as a Young Dog* (London: J. M. Dent & Sons, 1940)
DE	*Deaths and Entrances* (London: J. M. Dent & Sons, 1946)
Selected Writings	*Selected Writings of Dylan Thomas* (New York: New Directions, 1946)
ICS	*In Country Sleep* (New York: New Directions, 1952)
CP (Brit.)	*Collected Poems 1934-1952* (London: J. M. Dent & Sons, 1952)
CP (U.S.)	*The Collected Poems of Dylan Thomas* (New York: New Directions, 1953)
QE (Brit.)	*Quite Early One Morning* (London: J. M. Dent & Sons, 1954)
QE (U.S.)	*Quite Early One Morning* (New York: New Directions, 1954)

LVW   *Dylan Thomas: Letters to Ver-
                       non Watkins* (London: J. M.
                       Dent & Sons, and Faber &
                       Faber, 1957)

Manuscript Sources:

BBC   The British Broadcasting Corpo-
                       ration
BM   British Museum
Hanley   The collection of T. E. Hanley
M.I.T.   The Massachusetts Institute of
                       Technology
Notebook   Lockwood Library of the State
                       University of New York at
                       Buffalo

Periodicals:

Botteghe   *Botteghe oscure*
CP&P   *Contemporary Poetry and Prose*
LLT   *Life and Letters To-day*
NEW   *New English Weekly*
NS   *New Stories*
NV   *New Verse*
O'London's   *John O'London's Weekly*
SGSM   *Swansea Grammar School Maga-
                       zine*
S Ref   *Sunday Referee*
20thC Verse   *Twentieth Century Verse*

Appendix I

Chronology of Composition

> *"The opossums are un-satisfactory, I know."*
>
> Dylan Thomas to
> Vernon Watkins, 1938

THERE IS A MELANCHOLY CONVENIENCE in the fact that Dylan Thomas prepared his *Collected Poems* in the year before his death. The volume, like a last will and testament, contains all the poems that he wished to leave to the world. It is, in fact, a compilation of all five of his previously published volumes reproduced in sequence with very little alteration.[1] Scholars and critics thus have an apparently settled corpus by which to judge Thomas' development in style and subject matter. Unfortunately the definitiveness of the *Collected Poems*, as far as chronology is concerned, is more apparent than real. The order in which Thomas wrote his poems is quite different from the order in which they were published, so that statements about his development based on the sequence of the *Collected Poems* have had only limited validity.

The major source of information for the chronology of composition is the collection of Dylan Thomas' notebooks for the years 1930 to 1934 (with gaps), now at the Lockwood Memorial Library of the State University of New York at Buffalo.[2] Not only did Thomas date a poem when he first copied it into his notebook, but he also generally dated the revisions as he went back to the notebooks time and time again up to 1941. The poet's *Letters to Vernon Watkins* is the chief authority for the date of poems after the notebooks end in 1934. In surprisingly few cases are we left without circumstantial evidence to give a better date than that of first publication. The *Bibliography*, compiled by J. Alexander Rolph in 1956, has been invaluable throughout.

The poet's schoolboy publications for the most part are not serious, and are definitely inferior to other poems he was writing at the time.[3] By December 1930, when as editor of the *Swansea Grammar School Magazine* he printed his *Captain Bigger's Isle* (first line: "Captain Bigger was the skipper of the steamer *Duke of York*"), he had already composed the early versions of *How shall my animal* and *Today, this insect*. And before he left school at sixteen and a half he had written *The spire cranes* in a form close to its final published state in *The Map of Love* eight years afterwards.

The existence of such delayed publication of early poems is the most notable discovery to be made in the chronology. About half the poems in Thomas' two middle volumes, *Twenty-five Poems* (1936) and *The Map of Love* (1939), had their origin in that amazing burst of creativity in the two years prior to *18 Poems* (1934). Moreover, it is exactly these poems — some of them hardly revised at all — that are usually cited as indicating a trend toward clarity in Thomas' mid-career. "C.B.S." reviewing *Twenty-five*

Poems in *New Verse* (Christmas 1936) divided the volume into "sense" and "nonsense" poems: the nine "sense" poems are all early, revised poems.[4] We can now see that the "trend toward clarity" was really a recourse to early poems that Thomas had refrained from including in *18 Poems*.

While in the following Chronology emphasis is on Thomas' poetic output,[5] some attempt has been made to list prose and other writings, and to give biographical mileposts where they are known.

SCHOOLBOY POEMS

Born Swansea 27 October 1914. Entered Swansea Grammar School September 1925 (aged almost 11); left July 1931 (aged 16¾). An editor of the *SGSM* from July 1929. Publications there consist of 27 poems (including one later as an Old Boy), various parodies and notes, two short stories, and two essays: "Films" and "Modern Poetry." Schoolboy poems also appeared in *Western Mail* (14 January 1927) and *Boys Own Paper* (February 1927).

Thomas quotes from 5 of his early poems (c. 1929) in his story "The Fight" and from another in "Reminiscences of Childhood." In the BM are typescripts of 8 poems possibly pre-1930, including "third person plural" poems done in collaboration with Daniel Jones.[6]

Two lines from a poem submitted in a competition appear in *Everyman* (10 October 1929). Thomas was a winner of the BBC Poetry Competition in February 1933 with *The Romantic Isle* (not extant) broadcast 28 June 1933.

BUFFALO NOTEBOOKS

1930 Notebook: "Mainly Free Verse Poems" — numbered 1 to 42 (plus 4 deleted poems) from 27 April 1930 to 9 December 1930. The BM has typed copies of 18 of these poems. This Notebook contains the ancestor of *How shall my animal*.

1930-1932 Notebook: "Mainly Free Verse Poems" — numbered I to LVVVI (plus 6 unnumbered poems) from December 1930 to July 1932. The BM has typed copies of 9 and autographs of 2. This Notebook contains early versions of *To-day, this insect*, *The spire cranes*, *Why east wind chills*, *The Hunchback in the Park*, and *Out of the sighs*.

A Notebook for July 1932 to January 1933 is not extant, but certain poems possibly belong to this period: (1) 8 poems for which the BM has type-scripts, including an early version of *Especially when the October wind;* (2) early versions of such published poems as, possibly, *Once it was the colour of saying*, *When all my five and country senses see*, *Should lanterns shine*, *Then was my neophyte*, *That sanity be kept*, and *Do you not father me*.

February 1933 Notebook: "Poems" — numbered One to Fifty Three, from 1 February 1933 to 16 August 1933, with five gaps. The BM has typed copies of 5 poems, and autographs of 2; Hanley has typescripts of 7. This Notebook contains early versions of *Was there a time*, *After the funeral*, *On no work of words*, *I have longed to move away*, *On the Marriage of a Virgin*, *See, on gravel paths*, *O make me a mask*, *And death shall have no dominion*, *Out of the Pit*, *Not from this anger*, *First there was the lamb on knocking knees, We lying by seasand, In-carnate devil, No man believes, The tombstone told when she died, Why east wind chills, Greek Play in a Garden, Here in this spring, Find meat on bones, Ears in the turrets hear, The Woman Speaks,* and *Shall gods be said to thump the clouds.*

August 1933 Notebook: Numbered One to Forty One, from 17 August 1933 to 30 April 1934, with two gaps. The BM has typed copies of 5 poems; Hanley, 7. This Notebook contains versions of *The hand that signed the paper, That the sum sanity, Grief thief of time, The seed-at-zero, Before I knocked, My hero bares his nerves, In the beginning, Love me, not as the dreaming nurses, I fellowed sleep, The force that through the green fuse drives the flower, From love's first fever to her plague, When once the twilight locks no longer, Light breaks where no sun shines, This bread I break, A process in the weather of the heart, Foster the light, Our eunuch dreams, Where once the waters of your face, I see the boys of summer,* and *If I were tickled by the rub of love.*

Red Notebook: Ten short stories written between 28 December 1933 and October 1934: "The Tree," "Martha," "After the Fair," "The Enemies," "The Dress," "The Visitors," "The Vest," "Gaspar, Melchior, Balthasar," "The Burning Baby" and "Mr. Tritas On The Roofs" (or "Anagram").

SWANSEA JOURNALISM

On staff of *South Wales Daily Post:* first piece "Nellie Wallace's Mimicry" (15 July 1931); last piece "Genius and Madness Akin in World of Art" (7 January 1933). Thomas did 7 articles on local poets in *Herald of Wales;* a poem *Youth Calls to Age* accompanies that on 23 April 1932. *Herald of Wales* also published *Greek Play in a Garden* on 15 July 1933 (from Notebook 7 July 1933).

Swansea and West Wales Guardian published *That the sum sanity* on 8 June 1934 (revised from Notebook 24 August 1933), and several journalistic pieces.

London Publications Before 18 Poems

1. *NEW* 18 May 1933—*And death shall have no dominion* (from Notebook April 1933); revised in Notebook February 1936 for *25P.*

2. *Adelphi* September 1933 — *No man believes* (from Notebook 23 May 1933).

3. *S Ref* 3 September 1933—*That sanity be kept* (no MS extant).

4. *S Ref* 29 October 1933—*The force that through the green fuse drives the flower* (from Notebook 10 October 1933); reprinted *18P.*

5. *S Ref* 7 January 1934 — *Love me, not as the dreaming nurses* (from Notebook 18 September 1933).

6. *NEW* 25 January 1934—*Out of the Pit* (from Notebook 16-20 April 1933).

7. *S Ref* 11 February 1934—*A process in the weather of the heart* (from Notebook 2 February 1934); reprinted *18P.*

8. *Adelphi* March 1934—*The Woman Speaks* (from Notebook July 1933).

9. *Listener* 14 March 1934—*Light breaks where no*

sun shines (from Notebook 20 November 1933);
reprinted *18P.*

10. *NEW* 15 March 1934—"After the Fair" (from
Red Notebook November 1933).

11. *S Ref* 25 March 1934—*Where once the waters
of your face* (from Notebook 18 March 1934);
reprinted *18P.*

12. *NV* April 1934 — *Our eunuch dreams* (from
Notebook March 1934); reprinted *18P.*

Thomas' award of the Book Prize is in *S Ref*
22 April 1934. After several visits, Thomas took up
residence in London in November 1934 with periodic
"return journeys" to Swansea.

13. *O'London's* 5 May 1934—*Ears in the turrets hear*
(emended from Notebook 17 July 1933); full
version *25P.*

14. *NV* June 1934—*When once the twilight locks
no longer* (from Notebook 11 November 1933);
revised for *18P.*

15. *NV* June 1934—*I see the boys of summer* (from
Notebook April 1934); reprinted *18P.*

16. *NS* June-July 1934—"The Enemies" (from Red
Notebook 11 February 1934).

17. *NV* August 1934—*If I were tickled by the rub
of love* (from Notebook 30 April 1934); reprinted *18P.*

18. *Adelphi* September 1934—Reviews of poetry.

19. *Criterion* October 1934—*From love's first fever
to her plague* (from Notebook 17 October 1933);
reprinted *18P.*

20. *NV* October 1934—"Answers to an Enquiry."

21. *Listener* 24 October 1934—*Especially when the*

October wind (revised from BM version); re-printed *18P*.

22. *S Ref* 28 October 1934—*Foster the light* (from Notebook 23 February 1934); revised for *CP&P* May 1936, and reprinted *25P*.

23. *NEW* 22 November 1934—"The End of the River."

24. *Adelphi* December 1934 — "The Tree" (from Red Notebook 28 December 1933).

25. *NV* December 1934—*My world is pyramid* (no extant MS); reprinted *18P*.

26. *NV* December 1934—Review of Stephen Spender's "Vienna."

COMPOSITION OF 18 POEMS

Published 18 December 1934. In April 1934 Thomas' choice for his first volume was 9 poems published or about to be (items 4, 7, 8, 9, 11, 12, 14, 15 above, and *That the sum sanity* revised from its Swansea publication), plus two poems in the August 1933 Notebook, *Before I knocked* and *Not forever shall the lord of the red hail;* "and about 6 or 7 others." Thomas changed his mind about the last poem, about *That the sum sanity*, and about item 8, *The Woman Speaks*. As the book was delayed through the summer, Thomas wrote and included *If I were tickled by the rub of love* (item 17), *I dreamt my genesis* (c. May 1934), *All all and all the dry worlds lever* (c. July 1934), *My world is pyramid* (c. August 1934; item 25), and *When, like a running grave* (c. September 1934). To these were finally added items 19 and 21 above, and revisions from the August 1933 Notebook: *My hero bares his nerves* (17 September

1933), *In the beginning* (18 September 1933 and April 1934), and *I fellowed sleep* (5 October and 27 November 1933).

COMPOSITION OF TWENTY-FIVE POEMS

Published 10 September 1936.

1. *I, in my intricate image*—written c. December 1934-March 1935; published *NV* August-September 1935.

2. *Hold hard, these ancient minutes in the cuckoo's month*—probably written c. April-May 1935; published *Caravel* March 1936.

3. *A grief ago*—probably written May-June 1935.

4. *How soon the servant sun*—written for publication, with item 3, in *Programme* 23 October 1935.

5. *Now*—usually associated with item 4; first published *25P*.

6. *Do you not father me*—rewritten c. July 1935 from a version in typescript (c. October 1934); published *Scottish Bookman* October 1935.

7. *Incarnate devil*—from Notebook 16 May 1933; revised for *S Ref* 11 August 1935 (revision copied in Notebook 20 January 1936).

8(a). *Grief thief of time*—first stanza from Notebook 26 August 1933; revised in Notebook "Donegal August 1935."

9(a). *Altarwise by owl-light* (sonnets I-VII) — probably written Summer 1935; published *LLT* December 1935.

10. *The hand that signed the paper*—emended from Notebook 17 August 1933 for publication, with items 11 and 12, in *NV* December 1935.

11. *I have longed to move away*—revised from Note-

book 1 March 1933 (revision copied in Notebook 13 January 1936).
12. *Should lanterns shine*—probably from early version c. 1932.

Thomas was in Swansea preparing *25P* during
December 1935-February 1936, and completed the
following:

8(b). *Grief thief of time* — second stanza from
Notebook 26 September 1933, revised; whole
poem published *Comment* 1 February 1936.
9(b). *Altarwise by owl-light* (sonnets VIII-X)—
published *CP&P* May 1936 and July 1936.
13. *Was there a time*—from Notebook 8 February
1933; thorough revision in Notebook December
1935; published *NEW* 3 September 1936.
14. *Here in this spring*—from Notebook 9 July 1933;
thorough revision in Notebook January 1936;
first published *25P*.
15. *Find meat on bones*—from Notebook 15 July
1933; revision interlined January 1936; published
Purpose April-June 1936.
16. *Why east wind chills*—from Notebook 1 July
1933 (with ancestor 12 September 1931); thorough revision in Notebook 21 January 1936;
published *NEW* 16 July 1936.
17. *Foster the light* — from Notebook 2 February
1934; early version published *S Ref* 28 October
1934; rewritten for *CP&P* May 1936.
18. *This bread I break*—from Notebook 24 December 1933; published *NEW* 16 July 1936.
19. *The seed-at-zero*—early version in Notebook 29
August 1933; later version *25P*.

20. *Shall gods be said to thump the clouds*—from Notebook August 1933; thoroughly revised for *25P*.

21. *Out of the sighs*—from Notebook 7 June and 1 July 1932; revised for *25P*.

22. *Ears in the turrets hear*—from Notebook 17 July 1933; short version in *O'London's* 5 May 1934; full version *25P*.

23. *To-day, this insect*—early version in Notebook 18 December 1930; completely rewritten for *25P*, and published *Purpose* October-December 1936.

The volume was expanded from *Twenty-Three Poems*[7] by the addition of:

24. *Then was my neophyte* — possibly from early version c. 1932; published with item 23 above.

25. *And death shall have no dominion*—early version in Notebook April 1933; published *NEW* 18 May 1933; revision in Notebook February 1936; published *25P*.

OTHER PUBLICATIONS BETWEEN *18P* and *25P*

Poems not included in *25P*: *Poet: 1935* (from Notebook 31 March 1933) in *Herald of Wales* 8 June 1935; *Before we mothernaked fall* (from Notebook 16 September 1933) in *NEW* 30 July 1936.

Reviews in *Morning Post* (26), *Adelphi* (4), *Bookman* (1).

Stories later in *ML*: *Criterion* (2), *Comment* (1), *Transition* (1).

Other stories: "The Lemon" in *LLT* Spring 1936; "The Burning Baby" (from Red Notebook

September 1934) in *CP&P* May 1936; "The Horse's
Ha" in *Janus* May 1936; and "The School for
Witches" in *CP&P* August-September 1936.

COMPOSITION OF THE MAP OF LOVE

Proofs March 1939; published 24 August 1939.

1. *We lying by seasand*—from Notebook 16 May
   1933; revised for *Poetry* (Chicago) January
   1937; revision copied in Notebook September
   1937.
2. *It is the sinners' dust-tongued bell*—written 1936;
   published *20thC Verse* January 1937.

Married Caitlin Macnamara in Cornwall, July
1937. Resident alternatively at Blashford, Ringwood,
Hants, and at Laugharne, South Wales. Llewelyn
Thomas born January 1939.

A. "Exhausters"[8]
3. *I make this in a warring absence*—finished November 1937; published *20thC Verse* January-
   February 1938.
4. *How shall my animal*—finished March 1938 (ancestor in Notebook 9 December 1930); published
   Criterion October 1938.
5. *A saint about to fall* — finished October 1938;
   published *Poetry London* February 1939.
6. *'If my head hurt a hair's foot'*—finished March
   1939; published *Poetry London* April 1939.
B. "Opossums"[9]
7. *The spire cranes*—from Notebook 27 January
   1931; revised November 1937; published *Wales*
   March 1938 and *Poetry* (Chicago) August 1938,
   along with items 8, 9, and 10.

8. *O make me a mask*—from Notebook 31 March 1933; revised in Notebook November 1937.

9. *Not from this anger*—from Notebook 20 April 1933; revised in Notebook January 1938.

10. *When all my five and country senses see*—probably revised c. January 1938 from early version c. 1932.

11. *After the funeral*—from Notebook 10 February 1933; revised March-April 1938; published *LLT* Summer 1938.

12. *On no work of words*—from Notebook 16 February 1933; rewritten in Notebook September 1938; published *Wales* March 1939.

13. *The tombstone told when she died*—from Notebook July 1933; revised in Notebook September 1938; published *Seven* Winter 1938.

[not in *ML*] *I, the first named* — written October 1938; published *Seven* Winter 1938.

14. *Twenty-four years*—written October 1938; published *LLT* December 1938.

15. *Once it was the colour of saying*—written December 1938 (probably from early version c. 1932); published *Wales* March 1939.

16. *Because the pleasure-bird whistles*—written January 1939; published *20thC Verse* February 1939.

C. Stories

Most (probably all) of the stories in *ML* had their inception during 1933-34.[10] They were collected, with slight revision, from periodical publication: "The Visitor" (from Red Notebook April 1934) in *Criterion* January 1935; "The Enemies" (from Red Notebook 11 February 1934) in *NS* June-July 1934; "The Tree" (from Red Notebook 28 December

1933) in *Adelphi* December 1934; "The Map of Love" in *Wales* Autumn 1937; "The Mouse and the Woman" in *Transition* Fall 1936; "The Dress" (from Red Notebook March 1934) in *Comment* 4 January 1936; "The Orchards" (based on Red Notebook "Anagram" October 1934) in *Criterion* July 1936.

Except for the title story they were not among the prose pieces published since *25P:* "A Prospect of the Sea" in *LLT* Spring 1937; "The Holy Six" in *CP&P* Spring 1937; "Prologue to an Adventure" in *Wales* Summer 1937; "In the Direction of the Beginning" in *Wales* March 1938; "An Adventure from a Work in Progress" in *Seven* Spring 1939; "The True Story" and "The Vest" (from Red Notebook 20 July 1934) in *Yellow Jacket* May 1939.

Other prose: 10 fiction reviews for *NEW* between March 1938 and December 1939. Thomas' "Tribute to Auden" in *NV* November 1937 was probably written in February 1937.

COMPOSITION OF PORTRAIT

Proofs January 1940; published 4 April 1940. These stories, probably written immediately prior to publication, were collected with slight alteration: (1) "A Visit to Grandpa's" in *NEW* 10 March 1938; (2) "One Warm Saturday" — finished July 1938; (3) "The Peaches" *LLT* October 1938; (4) "Old Garbo" in *LLT* July 1939; (5) "Extraordinary Little Cough" in *LLT* September 1939. In August 1939 Thomas was working on the stories for a December 1939 deadline. (6) "Just Like Little Dogs" in *Wales* October 1939; (7) "The Fight" in *LLT* December 1939; (8) "Patricia, Edith, and Arnold" in *Seven* Christmas

1939; (9) "Where Tawe Flows"; and (10) "Who Do You Wish Was With Us?" — finished by early December 1939.

POETRY 1939

Thomas resident in Laugharne.

Unluckily for a Death — first version finished May 1939; published *LLT* October 1939; rewritten for *DE*.

To Others than You — written May 1939;[11] published *Seven* Autumn 1939 and *DE*.

When I Woke — written c. July 1939; published *Seven* Autumn 1939; revised for *DE*.

Paper and Sticks — written for publication in *Seven* Autumn 1939; reprinted *DE*, but not *CP*.

Once below a time — written December 1939; published *LLT* March 1940; not in *DE*, but reprinted *CP*.

WARTIME WRITING

At Blashford, January-April 1940; at Sea View, Laugharne, April-June 1940.

There was a Saviour — written January-March 1940; published *Horizon* May 1940 and *DE*.

The Countryman's Return — written March 1940; published *Cambridge Front* Summer 1940; not in *DE*.

Into her Lying Down Head — written March-June 1940; published *LLT* November 1940; slightly revised for *DE*.

At John Davenport's house, Marshfield, Wilts, June 1940-January 1941.

On a Wedding Anniversary — probably written July 1940; published *Poetry London* 15 March 1941; revised for *DE*.

Love in the Asylum — possibly written Summer 1940; published *Poetry London* May-June 1941 and *DE*.

Request to Leda — published *Horizon* July 1942; not in *DE*. This "Homage to William Empson" was one of the parodies in the unpublished satirical novel *The Death of the King's Canary* written with John Davenport c. July-August 1940.

BBC scripts for Latin American Service: (1) "Duque de Caxias" August 1940; (2) "Cristobal Colon" October 1940; and (3) "March of the Czech Legion" — finished February 1941 (not used).

Deaths and Entrances — written c. September 1940; published *Horizon* July 1942 and *DE*.

At parents' home, Bishopston, near Swansea, January-April 1941.

Ballad of the Long-legged Bait — begun in 1940, finished February 1941; published *Horizon* July 1941 and *DE*.

On the Marriage of a Virgin — from Notebook 22 March 1933; revised in Notebook January 1941; further revision June-July 1941; published *LLT* October 1941 and *DE*.

At Richard Hughes' Laugharne Castle, May-August 1941.

"Adventures in the Skin Trade" — initiated August 1940, written mainly May-June 1941; first section published *Folios of New Writing* Autumn

1941, remaining sections *New World Writing* November 1952 and May 1953.

Among those Killed in the Dawn Raid was a Man Aged a Hundred — written July 1941; published *LLT* August 1941 and *DE*.

The Hunchback in the Park — from Notebook 9 May 1932; revised in Notebook 16 July 1941; published *LLT* October 1941 and *DE*.

London and environs, August 1941-June 1944.

A Dream of Winter—poem commissioned by *Lilliput* for photo captions January 1942.

Film scripts include: (1) "These Are the Men," released April 1943; (2) "The Three Weird Sisters"; (3) Lockwood MSS: "The Unconquerable People"; a documentary on a girls' reformatory; and a film synopsis of Maurice O'Sullivan's *Twenty Years A Growing*; (4) "Our Country" — published *Wales* Autumn 1943; and (5) "The Doctor and the Devils" — finished October 1944, prepared for publication 1947, published 1953.

BBC performances as actor/reader on 19 September 1941, 25 May 1942, 29 November 1942, and 8 August 1943. "Reminiscences of Childhood" — written for BBC Wales broadcast 15 February 1943; published *Listener* 25 February 1943 and *QE*

Last night I dived my beggar arm and *Your breath was shed* — probably written from early versions; published *Poetry London* c. April 1944; not in *DE*.

Ceremony After a Fire Raid — finished for publication in *Our Time* May 1944; in *DE*.

Carmarthen, July - September 1944; Newquay, Cardiganshire, September 1944-September 1945.

Poem in October — possibly begun in Laugharne, October 1939; finished August 1944; published *Horizon* February 1945.

Vision and Prayer — finished August 1944 (probably begun for daughter's birth a year before); published *Horizon* January 1945.

Holy Spring — finished November 1944; published *Horizon* January 1945.

"Quite Early One Morning" — written for BBC Wales; recorded 14 December 1944, broadcast 31 August 1945; published *Wales* Autumn 1946.

The following poems were finished in the period prior to the proofs of *DE*, December 1944-April 1945:

A Winter's Tale — in *Poetry* (Chicago) July 1945.

A Refusal to Mourn the Death, by Fire, of a Child in London — in *New Republic* 14 May 1945 and *Horizon* October 1945.

Lie Still, Sleep Becalmed — in *LLT* June 1945.

This Side of the Truth and *The Conversation of Prayer* — in *LLT* July 1945.

Fern Hill — in *Horizon* October 1945.

In My Craft or Sullen Art — in *LLT* October 1945.

Deaths and Entrances (book) — published 27 February 1946.

Poet as Performer

Chelsea, October 1945-March 1946; Holywell Ford, Oxford, March 1946-April 1947

Thomas did about 50 broadcasts in this period

as reader, mainly for John Arlott in BBC Eastern Service. Specially written broadcasts were:

1. "Memories of Christmas" — BBC Wales 16 December 1945; published *Listener* 20 December 1945 and *QE* (Brit.); revised for *Harper's Bazaar* December 1950 and *QE* (U.S.);

2. "Welsh Poets" — BBC Eastern 5 January 1946; in *QE;*

3. "On Poetry" — BBC Light 18 June 1946 — discussion with James Stephens; appears in part in *QE;*

4. "This is London" — BBC African 15 July 1946;

5. "Wilfred Owen" — BBC Eastern 27 July 1946; in *QE;*

6. "How to Begin a Story" — BBC Home 8 October 1946; published *Listener* 17 October 1946 and *QE;*

7. "What has happened to English Poets?" — BBC North American 16 October 1946 — a discussion;

8. "Holiday Memory" — BBC Wales 25 October 1946; published *Listener* 7 November 1946 and *QE;*

9. "Walter de la Mare as a Prose Writer" — BBC Third 30 November 1946; published *Living Writers*, ed. G. H. Phelps (1947), and *QE;*

10. "The Crumbs of One Man's Year" — BBC Home 27 December 1946; published *Listener* 2 January 1947 and *QE;*

11. "Oxford-Princeton"—BBC North American, recorded 29 December 1946;

12. "Sir Philip Sidney" — BBC West of England 24 January 1947; in *QE;*

13. "Return Journey" — written February 1947 for BBC Home, recorded 2 April 1947, broadcast 9 May 1947; in *QE*.

Thomas answered "Questionnaire" in *Horizon* September 1946.

Italian visit, April-August 1947.

In country sleep — begun in 1946, finished July 1947; published *Horizon* December 1947.

South Leigh, Oxford, September 1947-March 1949.

"Conversation About Christmas" — written for *Picture Post* 27 December 1947.

During this period Thomas did a further 50 broadcasts, notably reading Satan's part in *Paradise Lost*, W. H. Davies' *The Autobiography of a Supertramp*, and as a performer in several plays produced by Louis MacNeice. Specially written broadcasts were (1) "A Dearth of Comic Writers" — BBC Light 14 February 1948 — discussion with Arthur Calder-Marshall; in part in *QE*; and (2) "The English Festival of Spoken Poetry" — BBC Third 30 July 1948; published *Listener* 5 August 1948 and *QE*.

Address to Scottish P.E.N.; published *Voice of Scotland* December 1948.

Film script: "The Beach of Falesa" — written 1948; published posthumously *Harper's Bazaar* August 1959.

Resident in Laugharne from April 1949.

Over Sir John's hill — written in Laugharne; published *Botteghe* December 1949.

Specially written broadcasts: (1) "Living in Wales" — BBC Scottish 23 June 1949; (2) "On Edward Thomas" — BBC Wales 29 July 1949; (3) "On Reading One's Own Poems" — BBC Third 24 September 1949; in *QE;* and (4) "Swansea and the Arts" — BBC Wales 24 October 1949.

Stage appearance in reading of William Blake's "An Island in the Moon," produced by Eric Capon 16 February 1950.

"How to Be a Poet" — written for *Circus* April 1950 and May 1950.

1st visit to U. S., 21 February to 31 May 1950.

In the white giant's thigh — finished by September 1950; published *Botteghe* 1950 with a note.

Broadcasts: (1) "Three Poems" — BBC Third 25 September 1950; in *QE;* (2) "Poetic Licence" — BBC Home 13 December 1950 — discussion with George Barker, Roy Campbell, and W. R. Rodgers; (3) "Persian Oil" — BBC Home 17 April 1951 — written after a visit to Persia, January 1951; (4) "The Festival Exhibition 1951"—BBC Wales 19 June 1951; in *QE*. There were 11 other broadcasts as actor/reader in this period.

Poem on his Birthday — presumably begun October 1949, finished July 1951; published *World Review* October 1951.

Do not go gentle into that good night — possibly begun 1945; finished by July 1951; published *Botteghe* 1951.

Lament — possibly written c. July-August 1951; published *Botteghe* 1951; revised for *ICS*.

"Llareggub (A Piece for Radio Perhaps)" — in progress spring and summer 1951; published *Botteghe* 1952.

In Country Heaven (unpublished poem) — probably finished c. October 1951.

In Country Sleep (book) — compiled c. November 1951 for publication 28 February 1952.

Review of Roy Campbell's *Light on a Dark Horse* in *Observer* 16 December 1951.

2nd visit to U. S., 15 January to 16 May 1952.

"I am Going to Read Aloud" — introduction to readings, recorded M.I.T. 7 March 1952; published posthumously *London Magazine* September 1956.

Review of Amos Tutuola's *The Palm-Wine Drinkard* in *Observer* 6 July 1952.

Author's Prologue — written for *CP*; broadcast 26 October 1952; in *Listener* 6 November 1952.

Introduction and Selections from Edgar Lee Masters' *Spoon River Anthology* — written summer 1952; broadcast posthumously 23 January 1955; published *Harper's Bazaar* June 1963.

"The Followers" — in *World Review* October 1952.

Collected Poems (Brit.) published 10 November 1952.

Father's death, December 1952.

BBC readings: (1) poetry of Robert Lowell and Theodore Roethke, recorded 16 July and 1 August 1952; Lowell broadcast 14 October 1952; (2) Vernon Watkins' *Three Ballads* 14 January 1953; (3) four "Anthologies" produced by Aneirin Talfan Davies, BBC Wales, broadcast 1, 8, 15, 22 March 1953; and (4) "A Painter's Studio," BBC Television April 1953; published *Texas Quarterly* Winter 1961.

William Foyle Poetry Prize, January 1953.

3rd visit to U. S., 16 April to 3 June 1953.

Under Milk Wood — first solo reading 3 May 1953, Cambridge, Mass.; first cast performance 14 May 1953, New York Poetry Center; published post-humously *Mademoiselle* February 1954 and *Observer* 7 and 14 February 1954.

"A Visit to America" — introduction for readings, recorded M.I.T. 11 May 1953; rewritten for BBC recording 28 September 1953; broadcast posthumously 30 March 1954; published *Listener* 22 April 1954 and *QE*.

"The International Eisteddfod" — written for BBC Wales 13 July 1953; in *QE*.

"A Story" — written for BBC Television 10 August 1953; published *Listener* 17 September 1953 and *QE* (U.S.).

"Laugharne" — written for BBC Wales, recorded 5 October 1953, broadcast 5 November 1953; in *QE*.

4th visit to U. S., arrived 19 October 1953, died 9 November 1953.

At time of death Thomas was working on *Elegy*, published posthumously *Encounter* February 1956.

It is impossible in a short space to indicate the degree of conjecture or certainty in dating works and events. One problem that should be discussed is typified by *When all my five and country senses see*, a short poem in *ML* which seems of early vintage but for which there is no extant MS. On what basis may we categorize it as a revised poem? One main argument is from style: it is short, rather languid in tone, and easeful compared with the poems of major effort. Line-breaks are handled with a natural flair. Note the fanciful, almost flippant, imagery of the first ten lines, where the five senses are gaily interchanged:

> When all my five and country senses see,
> The fingers will forget green thumbs and mark
> How, through the halfmoon's vegetable eye,
> Husk of young stars and handfull zodiac,
> Love in the frost is pared and wintered by,
> The whispering ears will watch love drummed
>   away
> Down breeze and shell to a discordant beach,
> And, lashed to syllables, the lynx tongue cry
> That her fond wounds are mended bitterly.
> My nostrils see her breath burn like a bush.

"The whispering ears will *watch*" and "My nostrils *see*" — in a weightier poem such forced transpositions of the senses would be torn and twisted in the relentlessly changing imagery; here there is a consistency. The idea is stated in the first line: we are to imagine all our five senses as *seeing*. What each sees is the downfall of love in its own particular area, Love being a continent with a country for each sense. This fact in itself betrays the poem's minor status, the fact that it has a simple central conceit, "just a curious thought said quickly," as Thomas remarked about a previous minor poem.[12] The final four lines, which reveal the poem to be quite a regular sonnet, complete the thought: the heart is to be imagined as energizing a substitute for the other senses, a sixth sense capable of alone taking over the domain of love:

> My one and noble heart has witnesses
> In all love's countries, that will grope awake;
> And when blind sleep drops on the spying senses,
> The heart is sensual, though five eyes break.

Thomas is saying that the heart is the real, bountiful source of sensual love. This kind of ingenious conceit, which might supply a single line in a major poem, indicates a juvenile effort when it motivates the whole.

The argument from style and content is backed up by other considerations. For one thing, *When all my five and country senses see* was published alongside three revised poems, *The spire cranes*, *O make me a mask*, and *Not from this anger*, in *Poetry* (Chicago) August 1938, in which Thomas had published another juvenile poem, *We lying by seasand*, the previous year. To add to this guilt by association, we have evidence in the letters to Vernon Watkins. Four months after sending *The spire cranes* to Watkins, Thomas forwarded another batch of poems to be typed. "Here are 4 poems," he writes, himself distinguishing the major from the minor, "two short simple ones, done fairly quickly, a conventional sonnet, and one I have spent a great deal of time on."[13] *O make me a mask* and *Not from this anger* were two of the poems, the "short simple ones." The long poem was *How shall my animal*. This leaves the "conventional sonnet," which can only be *When all my five and country senses see*. Though Watkins' note does not quite jibe,[14] Thomas confirms in his next letter that he had sent that poem along with the others in the previous one:

> The opossums are unsatisfactory, I know. Before your letter came, I had cut out the ubiquitous "weather" from the anticlimactic poem, and am revising it all; I will conquer "rebellion in"; and "eyed" tongue shall, momentarily, become "lashed."[15]

Here Thomas is promising to revise the batch of smaller poems. Apparently they were sent off to *Poetry* without revision: the "weather" appears there in *Not from this anger*, and "rebellion in" in *O make me a mask*. There is no "eyed" tongue in these two poems, nor any sign of such a thing in their draft versions. "Eyed tongue" is in the *Poetry* printing of *When all my five and country senses see:* "And, lashed to syllables, the eyed tongue talk" (line 8). There can be little doubt, therefore, that this poem is the "conventional sonnet" previously mentioned, and consequently one of the "opossums" of the minor strain.

The opus was *How shall my animal*, a poem which poses another problem of categorization. Though it has a very early version in the 1930 Notebook, the sheer amount of effort the poet expended on it later — transformation a better word here than revision — forces the poem into the opus category. "I had worked on it for months," he told Watkins on 1 April 1938. The result is one of his most complicated and unyielding poems.[16] *After the funeral* is another crux. It had a series of preliminary drafts, beginning with twenty-five lines in the February 1933 Notebook, where it is not about any specific person. On the death of his aunt, Thomas turned the poem into a personal elegy. The draft that he sent to Watkins had fifteen lines. For the final version he added a long parenthesis in the middle of the poem; and a new ending came, according to Watkins, "in a rush." This last comment, added to the poet's reliance on the early draft for ideas and phrasing, makes it impossible to classify *After the funeral* with the laboriously worked poems of Thomas' main stream. Again the poet himself suggests the correct value judgment: "I'm making it longer and, I hope, better than any of my recent simple poems."[17] The implication is, however, that it is basically one of them.

Similar arguments are available for the few other doubtful cases.[18] *Twenty-four years*, the poet's October birthday poem for 1938, is a crossroads. Thomas admits it is built on a single line from an early (non-extant) poem.[19] But one feels that the poem is new, a new strong statement — a twenty-fourth birthday poem not an eighteenth. *Because the pleasure-bird whistles*, written for the New Year 1939, poses the same problem. When we see Thomas writing fairly straightforward poems not from laziness but from an apparently conscious effort to achieve a maximum effect in a new way, then we must logically discard the two categories, major and minor. It is as though Thomas had warmed to the idea of writing clearer poems. The revising of old poems, while obviously not in the main stream of Thomas' development, seems to have produced a change in the main stream. The result is a line of major and unobscure poems.

This is the probable truth about the trend toward clarity in Thomas' middle period. Because of the practical need to increase his output of poems to more than one a year, Thomas turned out the "opossums," which, to use his own word, were "unsatisfactory." The notebooks help us to see why they are unsatisfactory: to put it bluntly, he was reversifying old poems. It is the so-called difficult poems of this period that are the product of Thomas' full powers and most serious effort. At the same time, Thomas could not have helped realizing that the lesser poems were successful in a way his "exhausters" were not. We can presume, then, that he was led to develop a new conscious style, one which grows to perfection in *This Side of the Truth* and *In My Craft or Sullen Art*, careful poems of Thomas' highest effort.

Appendix II

Textual Cruxes

*"P.S. It's a full stop after
'ice' in the last verse."*

Dylan Thomas to
Vernon Watkins,
13 November 1937

THOMAS' PREFATORY "Note" to the *Collected Poems* has been taken to imply that he prepared a definitive text. But, as Appendix I showed, that volume was indeed a mere *collected* poems, very little selection or editing having occurred. The few slight changes seem inconsequential or even accidental. A few misprints were corrected in the later printings of the volume; a few still remain. These are taken up here, along with any other cruxes which might be thought to require emendation.

This is not to say that the *Collected Poems* is a bad text; on the contrary, it is extremely good. But studying Dylan Thomas is difficult enough without having to worry about the reliability of the text. The aim of this Appendix is to settle a few of our suspicions, by taking up all the cases that have come to light. It may be assumed that the English and American texts are identical unless otherwise stated.

Author's Prologue
l. 24 — *Listener* and several MSS have "strangers" set

off by commas. The less urgently vocative *CP* version seems preferable.

l. 51 — to be followed by a stanza break, not totally clear in *CP* (U.S.), though the later printings of *CP* (Brit.) doubly emphasize it by numbering the lines 1 to 51 and 51 to 1.

I see the boys of summer
I, ll. 3 & 20 — the commas, not present in MS or periodical printing, are unnecessary but inoffensive.

When once the twilight locks no longer
l. 3 — *NV*, *18P*, and *Selected Writings* all have "dammed." The "damned" of *CP* is a pun that one would wish to save Thomas from. Unfortunately it exists in the Notebook version 11 November 1933; and, writing to Vernon Watkins on 27 April 1946, he includes the phrase: "locked in these damned days. . . ."

Our eunuch dreams
II, l. 8 — *CP* (U.S.) has "showing"; apparently a misprint for "throwing" in *CP* (Brit.) and all other versions, including MSS.

When, like a running grave
ll. 42 & 44 — *CP* adds a superfluous comma after the parentheses; early typescript had commas but not the parentheses; *18P* had parentheses but not the following commas.

From love's first fever to her plague
l. 11 — followed in *18P* by a line omitted in *CP*:
    "And to the miracle of the first rounded word,"
— probably a deliberate deletion.
l. 18 — the internal comma was changed to a semi-

colon by the editor of *Criterion*, also the final comma
of l. 23 — both felicitous emendations.

Light breaks where no sun shines
l. 16 — *Listener* is strictly correct in omitting the
comma after "fenced." Notebook and *18P* has the
comma; but an early typescript does not.

I fellowed sleep
l. 4 — the apostrophe in *18P* " 'planing-heeled" serves
to explain the image.

I dreamed my genesis
l. 4 — an end comma would allow the "I" subject to
be brought down for the verb "shuffled" (l. 5), which
is otherwise without a subject.

My world is pyramid
l. 20 — the internal comma is puzzling, perhaps best
omitted? *NV* had a semicolon, which was more confusing still.

I, in my intricate image
II, l. 8 — periodical printing, supported by two MSS,
has "the Cadaverous gravels" in keeping with the cap-
italized "Cadaver" of III, l. 31.
II, l. 18 — one MS gives authority for an end comma.
As it stands with a semicolon (or with the period of
the first printing) the previous stanza has no finite
main verb, and the "Bring" becomes vocative rather
than (better) the transitive main verb.

This bread I break
l. 6 — early printings of *CP* (Brit.) had misprint
"wind" (taken from *25P*), later corrected to "wine."

Out of the sighs
l. 19 — followed in Notebook and early typescript by a line omitted in *25P* and *CP:* "And, sleeping, made me dream" — which explains the grammatical construction of the following phrase, "How much was happy," which, as it now stands, is awkwardly dependent on "Feeling."

A grief ago
l. 17 — the omission of the end comma in *Programme* is the one variant that pleases.

How soon the servant sun
l. 1 *et al.* — in *Programme* dashes set off the parenthetical passages; *25P* supplied parentheses and omitted the commas in ll. 1, 2, 3, 5, 9, 12, and 24. Strangely *CP* restored the unnecessary commas.

Ears in the turrets hear
ll. 12 & 22 — superfluous commas, only appropriate if there are also commas after "island" (l. 10) and "ships" (l. 21) as in MS.

Foster the light
l. 25 — superfluous comma in *CP*, not present in periodical printing or *25P*.

I have longed to move away
l. 8 — *CP* (U.S.) has misprint "From" instead of "For" in all other printings.

Grief thief of time
l. 22 — the *Comment* variant "to-day" is plausible but almost certainly not correct.

Altarwise by owl-light
Sonnet IV
l. 8 — "boy" was "lad" in *25P* and periodical printings; the apparently inconsequential change breaks
the off-rhyme scheme.
l. 10 — *CP* (U.S.) has misprint "shrowd" ("shroud"
in all other printings).
l. 11 — first printing in *LLT* had "Love's a reflection
of the mushroom features," thus making clear the
verbal status of the " 's," which, as it stands in *25P*
and *CP*, can easily be taken for a possessive, leaving
the sentence apparently without a main verb.
Sonnet V
l. 5 — both periodical printing and *25P* have end
comma; both have end semicolon in l. 10: neither
variant seems to clear up the punctuation problem in
this sonnet.
Sonnet VIII
l. 12 — this famous line was "Unsex my skeleton . . ."
in its periodical printing, an illuminating variant.

I make this in a warring absence
ll. 37-38 — *CP* (Brit.) puts these two lines with the
lines following, thus violating the stanzaic pattern
preserved in MS and other printings.

Not from this anger
l. 7 — followed by stanza break in Notebook and
periodical printing; in *ML* a page division obscures
this fact.

The tombstone told when she died
l. 10 — followed by stanza break in versions up to
ML, which again obscures this fact because of pagination.

'If my head hurt a hair's foot'
l. 19 — "none" repeated only once in the version sent to Vernon Watkins and printed in *Kenyon Review*. The third Hopkensian "none" appears in *Poetry London* and *ML*.

The Conversation of Prayer
l. 18 — *CP* (U.S.) has "his made grave" following Hanley MS, *LVW*, and *New Republic*; *CP* (Brit.) has "his true grave" following *LLT* and *DE*.

To Others than You
ll. 18-19 — *Seven* printing adds comma after "That"; the version in *LVW* omits the end comma of l. 19: either alternative is more strictly correct than *CP*.

Into her Lying Down Head
II, l. 19 — *LLT* and *LVW* have "Celebrating at his side" — a reading appropriate to the sense.

Do not go gentle into that good night
l. 5 — early printings of *CP* (Brit.) had "has forked" following a typescript; later corrected to "had forked."

Ceremony After a Fire Raid
l. 18 — followed in *Our Time* by a one-word line: "Give" — omitted in *War Poets* (1945) and subsequent printings, leaving the poem rather misshapen.

Once below a time
I — the roman numeral "I" missing in *CP* (U.S.).

When I Woke
l. 19 — "death-stagged"—probably a deliberate emendation (along with others) from "death-staggered" in periodical printing.

Ballad of the Long-legged Bait
l. 77 — "smoothe" is a strictly incorrect form for the verb.
l. 107 — "Sussanah's" appeared in *CP* over proofreader's query; *Horizon* had correct "Susannah's."

Lament
l. 44 — *CP* (U.S.) has "Slung"; all other sources have "Slunk."

In the white giant's thigh
l. 20 — followed by new page in *CP* (Brit.); probably *CP* (U.S.) should show stanza break, which appears in periodical printing and *ICS*.
l. 56 — *CP* (Brit.) still prints "desires" following *ICS* instead of "desirers" which has MS authority as well as that of other printings.

At least one obvious mistake in "The Visitor" should be added: the girl Rhianon was called Millicent in an earlier draft; this name was left unchanged on one occasion on about the third page of the story.

Notes

CHAPTER I

1. Portrait by Bill Brandt, *Harper's Bazaar* LXXXVIII (February 1954), p. 129.

2. "Poetic Manifesto," *Texas Quarterly*, IV (Winter 1961), 48.

3. *Ibid.*, p. 47. At M.I.T. in 1952 he added Robert Service, Stevenson, Eskimo Nell, the *Boys Own Paper*, Keats, Burns, and Dostoevsky to the list; see "I am Going to Read Aloud," *London Magazine*, III (September 1956), 14.

4. Daniel Jones, "Dylan Thomas: Memories and Appreciations," *Encounter*, II (January 1954), 10; in E. W. Tedlock, ed., *Dylan Thomas: the Legend and the Poet* (London: Heinemann Publishers, 1960), p. 17; and in John Malcolm Brinnin, ed., *A Casebook on Dylan Thomas* (New York: Thomas Y. Crowell, 1960), p. 281.

5. Geoffrey Grigson, "Recollections of Dylan Thomas," *London Magazine*, IV (September 1957), 40.

6. *Adelphi*, X (June 1935), 179-181. The scope and accomplishment of Thomas' brief bout of reviewing for *Adelphi* is remarkable: new poetry by Soutar, Montgomerie, and Salt (September 1934), Gandhi's devotional lyrics (January 1935), new poetry by Lyle Donaghy, John Lehmann, and Ruth Pitter (February 1935), a poetical tract by Alfred Haffenden (February 1935), the Clare (June 1935), and a survey of world literature by R. D. Jameson (October 1935).

7. The following list from a manuscript at the Lockwood Library, State University of New York at Buffalo, is apparently the fare, both humorous and serious, that Thomas was preparing for his audiences:

Poem—Yeats/Poem—Norman Cameron/Poem—Mcneice/ Chard Witlow—H Reed/Naming of Parts—H Reed/Potpourri from a Summer Garden—John Betjeman/2 Grotesques — Robert Graves / The Great Grandmother— Robert Graves/Hospital in Poona—Alun Lewis/Have I a Wife—LAG Strong/Carol—John Short/Poem—William Morgan/Poem—Edward Thomas/Poem—Walter de la Mare/Poem—Vernon Watkins/Poem—W. H. Auden/

Poem—W. S. Graham/Poem—George Barker/Poem—Ruth Pitter/Waterfall—Norman Nicholson/Poem—Bernard Spencer / Poem — Hardy / Blake / Herbert / Smart / Peele/Hopkins/D. H. Lawrence—Ship of Death/Browning/Wm. Barnes/Frank O'Connor translation/John Clare (Foolish, fond)/Vaughan

8. "I am Going to Read Aloud," *London Magazine*, III (September 1956), 14. Thomas would have seen Norman Cameron's translation of *Bateau ivre* in *New Verse* (June-July 1936); and certainly the *Ballad of the Long-legged Bait* is like Rimbaud's poem. But, after Thomas' pointed remark, there seems no reason to take general similarities as indicating "a faithful parody of *Bateau ivre*," as William York Tindall puts it in *The Literary Symbol* (New York: Columbia University Press, 1955), p. 155, or to speak of the *Ballad* as "deriving almost certainly from Rimbaud's *Bateau ivre*" as Derek Stanford does in *Dylan Thomas: A Literary Study* (London, Neville Spearman, 1954; New York, Citadel Press, 1954), p. 119. See also Henry Treece, *Dylan Thomas: 'Dog Among the Fairies'* (2d ed.; London: Ernest Benn; New York: de Graff, 1956), pp. 45-46. There have been plenty of sea journeys. The most striking characteristic of the *Ballad* is the allegorizing of the sexual life-cycle: a girl-bait on the man's fishing rod being made love to by a host of sea creatures until a climax is reached and the boat returns to land. If a parallel for this central allegorical action were to be found, then we could begin to talk of sources. *Bateau ivre* is no such analogue. One is indebted to Raymond Garlick's editorial in *Dock Leaves*, V (Spring 1954), 4, for reference to a stanza from Donne's *The Baite:*

> When thou wilt swimme in that live bath,
> Each fish, which every channell hath,
> Will amorously to thee swimme,
> Gladder to catch thee, than thou him.

Here is a partial parallel. But since Donne's image goes no further than this, being merely a lover's conventional compliment, these four lines can hardly be considered a source. In *A Reader's Guide to Dylan Thomas* (New York: the Noonday Press, 1962), p. 251, William York Tindall is less insistent on the parody: "But reading seems unnecessary for an image so inevitable as this for all the caught."

9. An examination of the *Ballad* work sheets at the Lockwood Library was made by Patricia Earle Speyser in an unpublished M.A. thesis (State University of New York at Buffalo, 1959).

10. John L. Sweeney, Introduction to *Selected Writings of Dylan Thomas* (New York: New Directions, 1946), p. xvi.

11. David Aivaz, "The Poetry of Dylan Thomas," *Hudson*

Review, III (Autumn 1950), 401. G. S. Fraser in *Dylan Thomas* (London: Longmans, Green, 1957), p. 14, makes a similar connection between Rilke and *Should lanterns shine*.

12. *Dylan Thomas: Letters to Vernon Watkins* (London: J. M. Dent & Sons, and Faber & Faber, 1957), p. 105; hereafter cited as *LVW*. A passing reference to Rilke in a review in *Adelphi*, IX (February 1935), 318, is still later than the poems in question.

13. This does not exhaust, of course, the question of literary influences on Thomas. It merely suggests that the onus is on those who wish to show such influences. The matter has been taken up at length by Giorgio Melchiori in *The Tightrope Walkers* (London: Routledge & Kegan Paul, 1956). Melchiori gives an initial nod to the accepted influences on Thomas: Welsh, the Bible, Hopkins, Joyce (p. 222); but his subsequent discussion repudiates the influences one by one in finding basic differences instead of similarities. There is evidence in letters that the poet most highly regarded by the young Thomas was William Blake. Thomas wanted to be a "mystical" poet. References are made to Blake at various times in the ensuing chapters, but no attempt will be made to hold up Blake as a "source."

14. For the second edition of his book, Henry Treece left out entirely the section dealing with Welsh influence — perhaps on the advice of Glyn Jones, whose authority on Welsh forms he had used. In *Dock Leaves*, V (Spring 1954), 25, Glyn Jones writes:

> My friend Henry Treece in his book . . . gives several examples of what he believes to be *cynghanedd* in Dylan's poetry. Tambimuttu in numbers 11 and 13 of *Poetry London* makes similar claims on behalf of Welsh influences. Miss Kathleen Raine, writing in *The New Statesman* at the time of the poet's death, uses words which I feel must mean that she too credits him with a knowledge of Welsh metrics. My own view is that any traces of *cynghanedd* in Dylan Thomas's poetry derive not from a direct study of Welsh prosody, but are present either by accident or as a result of the influence upon him of Hopkins, whose knowledge of this involved subject was considerable.

15. I am indebted to Meredydd Evans for pointing out one example of *cynghanedd* in Thomas (perhaps the only one, and almost certainly accidental), l. 11 of the first part of *Vision and Prayer:*

To the *burn* / and *turn* / of *time,

which is a most casual line of English poetry compared with the Hopkins:

The down-*dugged* / *ground-*hugged* / *grey.

Thomas stated his own attitude to the "bardic forms" in "Welsh Poets" written for the BBC in 1946, in *Quite Early One Morning* (London: J. M. Dent & Sons, 1954), pp. 149-150; (New York: New Directions, 1954), p. 112; hereafter cited as *QE*.

> These forms rely on a great deal of assonance and alliteration and most complicated internal rhyming; and these effects in English have, in the hands of the few who have attempted to use them, succeeded only in warping, crabbing, and obscuring the natural genius of the English language.

See also Aneirin Talfan Davies, "A Question of Language," *Yr Einion*, IV (1953), 27.

16. Daniel Jones in Tedlock, p. 18. It is the syllabic nature of the stanza forms of *Vision and Prayer* that makes the achievement there quite different from that in George Herbert's *Easter Wings*, which hugs the safety of the iambic line. The Vision stanza goes from 1 to 9 syllables and back to 1 (the reverse of this in the Prayer stanza), each line rhythmically unique. Again there are lapses:

```
 I      1 2 3 4 5 6 7 8   9 8 7 6 5 4 3 2   1
        1 2 3 4 5 6 7 8   9 8 7 6 5 4 3 2   1
        1 2 3 4 5 6 7 8   8 8 7 6 5 4 3 2   1
        1 2 3 4 5 6 7 8   9 8 7 6 5 4 3 2   1
        1 2 3 4 5 6 7 _   9 8 7 5 4 3 2     1
        1 2 3 4 5 6 7 8  10 8 7 6 5 4 3 2   1
 II    10 8 7 6 5 4 3 2   1 2 3 4 5 6 8 8   9
        9 8 7 6 5 4 3 2   1 2 3 4 5 6 7 8   9
        9 8 7 6 4 4 3 2   1 2 3 4 5 6 7 8   9
        9 8 7 6 5 4 3 2   1 2 3 4 5 6 7 8  10
       11 8 7 6 6 5 4 3 2 1 2 3 4 5 6 7 8   9
        9 8 7 6 5 4 3 2   1 2 3 4 5 6 7 8   9
```

Most of the *18 Poems* are regularly iambic (the syllable count and the metrical beat go together in the pentameter). An exception is *I dreamed my genesis*. The syllable count is 12 7 10 8, and consistently so, while the rhythm is irregular:

> I dreamed my genesis in sweat of sleep, breaking
> Through the rotating shell, strong
> As motor muscle on the drill, driving
> Through vision and the girdered nerve.

From limbs that had the measure of the worm, shuffled
Off from the creasing flesh, filed
Through all the irons in the grass, metal
Of suns in the man-melting night.

These first two stanzas are enough to show the tight rhyme
scheme utilizing near-rhymes and the rhyming of accented with
unaccented syllable, e.g. *"driving:nerve," "metal:night," "journey:
man," "muzzled:gas,"* and so on. All these strictures smack of the
Welsh. But there is nothing like *Vision and Prayer* and *I dreamed
my genesis* in Welsh poetry. Though undeliberately Welsh in
some respects, they should be taken as completely unique.

17. The work sheets of *Over Sir John's hill* (47 sheets), along
with those of the *Author's Prologue* (94 sheets), were presented
to Harvard College Library in 1955 by Oscar Williams as a
memorial to Gene Derwood.

18. The count is

5	6	14	15	5	1	15	5	14	5	14	14
5	6	13	14	5	1	13	6	13	4	13	14
5	6	13	14	4	1	14	4	15	5	14	13
5	6	14	14	5	1	14	4	14	4	13	13
5	6	14	14	6	1	13	5	14	6	14	13

Into her Lying Down Head, of which Thomas said, "I've
never worked harder on anything, maybe too hard: I made it
such a difficult shape, too" *LVW*, p. 92), has a syllable count of
impressive consistency in its three stanzas as they now stand:

7	7	8	11	9	5	7	7	11	8	11	7	7	11	9	11	11	8	8	20	9	15	15
7	7	8	11	9	5	7	7	11	8	11	7	7	12	8	11	11	7	7	20	9	14	16
8	7	8	11	10	6	7	7	11	8	10	7	6	11	9	11	12	7	7	20	9	17	17

In an earlier printed version the long line in the last stanza had
nineteen syllables and was followed by five lines instead of three.
The revision was a normalization. With *Unluckily for a Death*,
on the other hand, revision meant loss of strict syllabic regularity
and rhyme-scheme, but the second version seems otherwise a
great improvement. It is hard to tell exactly what Thomas required of himself in this matter.

19. As reported by Marjorie Adix, "Dylan Thomas: Memories and Appreciations," *Encounter*, II (January 1954), 14; in Tedlock, p. 62; in Brinnin, *Casebook*, p. 286.

20. Marjorie Adix, in Tedlock, p. 63; in Brinnin, *Casebook*,
p. 287. I am indebted to Roberto Sanesi for retelling the story of
Thomas' reading habits during the summer months of 1947 on the
Island of Elba. Dylan, the story goes, spent each afternoon with

a different book, lying in the sun on a rock in the middle of the bay, and on finishing would throw the book into the sea.

21. As printed in *QE* (U.S.) p. 20. The earlier version appears in *QE* (Brit.), p. 21.

22. A revealing comment occurs in *LVW*, p. 82, where Thomas refers to the adjective "blacked" in *There was a Saviour*: "I had, quite apart (that is absurd, I mean secondarily to) from the poem, the blackout in mind."

23. I am indebted to A. E. Trick for his personal reminiscence that the inception of the poem was with some middle-aged men in business clothes whom Thomas saw wading on the seashore — "summer boys in their ruin." No particular of that epiphany survives in the final poem, unless briefly in the fourth stanza of part I. The "boys of summer" in the poem are not ruined men acting like boys but boys actively ruining.

CHAPTER II

1. Henry Treece, *Dylan Thomas: 'Dog Among the Fairies'* (London: Lindsay Drummond, 1949), p. 149. (This valuable appendix is not included in the second edition.)

2. *LVW*, p. 31.

3. The Notebook version of *Incarnate devil* (16 May 1933) at the Lockwood Library has an early try at the same image:

> Before we sinned we knew all evil,
> Hearing in snow that turned to ice
> The sibilant horror of the devil's voice.

4. Treece, 1st ed., p. 149.

5. Ralph N. Maud, "Obsolete and Dialect Words as Serious Puns in Dylan Thomas," *English Studies*, XLI (February 1960), 1-2.

6. "Answers to an Enquiry," *New Verse* (October 1934), p. 7.

7. Treece, 2d ed., p. 37. In the original letter, now in the Lockwood Library, the two sentences following the quoted passage are:

> Reading back over that, I agree it looks preciously like nonsense. To say that I "let" my images breed and conflict is to deny my critical part in the business.

He is anticipating and negating the implication that the poet is not in control of his poem.

8. *Ibid.*

9. In *New Verse* it is the "dog-dayed pulse / Of doubt and dark" that bursts in their throats.

10. *LVW*, p. 92.

11. "Celebrating at his side" — the line as sent to Vernon Watkins and as printed in *Life and Letters To-day* is surely correct: the enemy and the wife are at the husband's side.

12. *LVW*, p. 92.

13. Donald Davie, *Articulate Energy* (London: Routledge & Kegan Paul, 1955), p. 129.

14. *Ibid*, p. 126.

15. John Bayley, *The Romantic Survival* (London: Constable, 1957), p. 196.

16. A. D. S. Fowler, review in *Essays in Criticism*, VIII (January 1958), 83.

17. As reported by Marjorie Adix in Tedlock, p. 62; in Brinnin, *Casebook*, p. 285.

CHAPTER III

1. "Weathers" is not rare in Thomas. It is found in the early Jarvis stories of *The Map of Love*, and in the genesis poem, *In the beginning*:

> In the beginning was the mounting fire
> That set alight the weathers from a spark.

Also in *I, in my intricate image*:

> They climb the country pinnacle,
> Twelve winds encounter by the white host at pasture,
> Corner the mounted meadows in the hill corral;
> They see the squirrel stumble,
> The haring snail go giddily round the flower,
> A quarrel of weathers and trees in the windy spiral.

This stanza was in danger of slipping into the merely pastoral; but the word "weathers" gears it firmly to the world of process beneath the scenery. These are no pretty breezes moving the trees. A similar effect is achieved in *Hold hard, these ancient minutes in the cuckoo's month*:

> Down fall four padding weathers on the scarlet lands,
> Stalking my children's faces with a tail of blood.

The "weathers" belong to a beast, which uses them as claws, weapons of mortality and change, on the children. "Weathers" are the innumerable ever-changing facets of a state of existence; so that "wood of weathers" in *Altarwise* (sonnet II) and "the outside weathers" in *How shall my animal* are both periphrases for this mortal world, bringing in the special idea of being subject to process.

2. Josephine Miles, a pioneer in the field of word counts, has

attempted in *The Continuity of Poetic Language*, University of California Publications in English, XIX (1948-1951), pp. 304-402, to make critical judgments on the basis of frequency of words in a poet's work. One suspects, however, that her shrewd insights come more from reading the poets than from counting their words. The method of taking partial samples is invalid. In the case of Thomas, for instance, she counted adjectives, nouns, and verbs in the first 1,000 lines of *Selected Writings* (1946). But several words, listed because they occurred ten times or more turn up much less frequently later in the volume. "Face" and "word" occur only twice later, "bell" only once, and "tower" not at all; whereas "night," "water," and "bird" are used about twice as often as before. "Flesh" occurs eleven times in two poems not included in the *Selected Writings*. Using a complete count of the *Collected Poems*, we would have to emend Josephine Miles' list of Thomas' most-used words rather drastically. *Adjectives:* subtract two of the "rainbow colors" ("golden" and "red"); add several of what might be called eschatological adjectives: "long," "black," "old," "last," and "still." *Nouns:* subtract nine — "bell," "tower," "word," "land," "mouth," "voice," "weather," "boy," and "face"; add ten — "wind," "dark," "ghost," "fire," "flesh," "hill," "bed," "cloud," "star," and "wound." *Verbs:* subtract "drive" and "drop"; add several verbs of observation and utterance — "sing," "see," "cry," "hear" — as well as "die" and "come." These changes place Thomas' vocabulary very much more in line with that of his contemporaries. He has now 21 (rather than 17) of the 30 majority words of the 1940's; 15 (rather than 13) of the 37 minority words; 15 high-frequency words (rather than 11) shared with at least one other poet of the time; whereas words used with high frequency by Thomas alone are reduced from 12 to 10. The fact that the poet's total vocabulary, viewed statistically, differs so little from that of his fellow writers indicates the limited use of a total count in making literary judgements. Some refinement can be achieved by showing the most-used words in chronological groupings:

CP (3800 lines)	18P & 25P (1500 lines)	ML (400 lines)
man 90	man 53	love 14
love 89	time 47	eyes 12
sea 89	sea 41	heart 11
sun 82	death 38	stone 10
time 79	love 36	tongue 9
night 64	blood 34	sea 9
death 62	sun 32	red 8
dead 61	light 27	mouth 8
light 61	wind 27	black 8

heart 57	ghost 26	grave 8
blood 56	dead 25	lie 8
one 50	flesh 25	house 8

DE (1100 lines)	ICS (500 lines)
sun 33	night 23
sea 32	black 15
dark 27	hill 13
love 27	love 12
light 24	sun 12
dead 24	man 10
water 23	high 9
man 22	wood 9
birds 21	sleep 8
night 21	house 8
time 20	heron 7
heart 20	dew 7

His most-used words, it could be argued, reflect Thomas' pre-occupation during the four periods. 'Man" and "time" dominate the early volumes. The middle poems are more romantic with "love," "eyes," and "heart." *Deaths and Entrances* is a celebration of nature: "sun" and "sea." The very last poems are brooding: "night" and "black." What partial truth there may be in these summary comments is not proved by the word count — for several reasons. (1) The sample counted, even though it is the total possible, is not large enough to give the results statistical validity. (2) The list shows glaring contradictions. If *Deaths and Entrances* is so celebrational, why all the occurrences of "dark"? If the last poems are brooding, why "love" and "sun" so high on the list? (3) The count cannot take into consideration the chronology of composition, since so many of the poems are half-revised. (4) Finally and chiefly, no word count can reflect the several meanings of a single word. The numerical result shows Thomas to be a sea poet. But the sea from which dreams and corpses come, or to which Christmas memories roll, or through which the processes of nature operate, is quite different from the sea beside which lovers lie or in which the girl-bait is dragged. Only when certain words are found to be repeated to the same effect in the same group of poems can a count begin to confirm one's judgment about the type and quality of the vocabulary.

    3. *LVW*, p. 40.

    4. Treece, 2d ed., p. 37.

    5. It is never out of place to look at Blake in relation to Thomas' early poems. In "The fields from Islington to Marylebone" we find:

> He [Satan] withered up the Human Form
> By laws of sacrifice for Sin,
> Till it became a Mortal Worm,
> But O! translucent all within.

For a portrayal of man literally in his maggot, see Blake's frontispiece "What is Man" to *The Gates of Paradise*, reproduced in the Everyman edition of Blake, p. 292, a volume that the young Dylan almost certainly had access to.

6. Stanford, pp. 59-60.

7. "Heaven" was a later addition to the poem. The manuscript version had:

> Love drips and gathers, but the fallen blood
> Shall make her well.
> And I am dumb to tell the timeless sun
> How time is all.

"Shall make her well" is clearly positive; and "time is all" should be too. Time is the enemy of man, yes, but not of the "timeless" sun ("timeless clouds," as it was in another draft), which is thought of as everlasting, not subject to wearing down by time. Revision made the ending unequivocal.

8. If we need confirmation that the subject of *Our eunuch dreams* really is dreams and movies, the notebook version (Thirty Seven in the August 1933 Notebook) ends with a clear summary of the issues:

> Which is the dream, and which the photograph?
> And which is life, is death?
> This is the world which whispers in our breath:
> This is the world. Have faith.

Dreams and movies are indistinguishable, both are death. And the draft ends with the voice of reality. There was a "jarring" optimism even in the revised stanza, according to Thomas in a letter to Grigson; he offered his editor a "less false" alternative to "Have faith" in the words "Suffer the world to spin." But the poem was printed without the substitution.

9. A possible line would enclose: (1) *Find meat on bones* (July 1933), perhaps the first poem in the notebooks to have process as its subject. Thomas had talked about process in *Especially when the October wind* and *Here in this spring* before this; but here disparate imagery gives a sense of process. Antithesis throughout: Find meat on bones (+) that soon have none (−), etc. (2) *Ears in the turrets hear* (July 1933). A simple statement of constraint as opposed to release. (3) *Shiloh's seed* (August 1933). (4) *Before I knocked* (September 1933). This and the last poem utilize the conception of Christ to express the operation of forces. (5) *My hero bares his nerves* (September

1933). The flesh-spirit duality ("mortal ghost") applied to the poet's own self. (6) *In the beginning* (September 1933). The duality in a Genesis setting. (7) *Grief thief of time* (August 1933). Opposite of genesis; the waste of human material. (8) *From love's first fever to her plague* (October 1933). Process vocabulary gives added dimension to the development of the individual from conception through embryo to youth. (9) *Foster the light* (February 1934). Antithetical exhortation. (10) *Where once the waters of your face* (March 1934). The sea is an arena for interplay of forces. Negative condition, with previous positive condition expressed in the adverbial "where" clauses. (11) *When, like a running grave* (c. September 1934). Predominantly images of decline. (12) *I dreamed my genesis* (c. May 1934). Death and rebirth. (13) *My world is pyramid* (c. August 1934). (14) *I, in my intricate image* (1935). (15) *Do you not father me* (1934-35). (16) *Hold hard, these ancient minutes in the cuckoo's month* (1935).

CHAPTER IV

1. *LVW*, p. 44.

2. Sigmund Freud, *The Interpretation of Dreams* (London, 3d ed., 1937), p. 334. The italics are mine.

3. Thomas, "Answers to an Inquiry," *New Verse*, No. 11 (October 1934), p. 9.

4. Freud, pp. 336, 339.

5. *LVW*, p. 92.

6. As reported by Marjorie Adix, in Tedlock, p. 66; in Brinnin, *Casebook*, p. 288.

7. Treece, 1st ed., p. 149.

8. *Ibid.*, pp. 149-150.

9. There has been a tendency to read "cracked" in this line as a past participle. But an examination of the contextual syntax shows that "cracked" can be no other than the past tense verb, and that the line is a complete sentence: "Abaddon in the hangnail *did crack* from Adam." See Ralph N. Maud, "Thomas' Sonnet I," *Explicator*, XIV (December 1955), art. 16.

10. We cannot here ignore another key that has been offered, Elder Olson's astronomical interpretation of the sonnets, which takes up most of the sixth chapter of *The Poetry of Dylan Thomas* (Chicago: University of Chicago Press, 1954). If the constellation Hercules were really the main hero of the poems, as Olson postulates, then this would certainly be a major factor in making more oblique our approach to the Christian core. But Thomas' acquaintances have not revealed that the poet had a vital interest in star maps, nor does Olson suggest that such an interest exhibits itself anywhere in the poet's writings other than

the sonnets. His theory is based on internal indications only. When the opening lines of sonnet I,

> Altarwise by owl-light in the half-way house
> The gentleman lay graveward with his furies,

are taken by Olson to describe the constellation Hercules setting toward the west with Scorpius, Draco, and Serpens Caput, his neighboring "furies" in the night sky, we are being asked to agree that this interpretation not only fits the poem but is *demanded* by it — since there is no sound reason why it should otherwise occur to us. The burden of proof is unbearably great. When sonnet VIII ("This was the crucifixion on the mountain") states quite definitely its subject matter, when Biblical references in every sonnet suggest a religious and specifically Christian theme, and when we have the gentleman called five lines later "that gentleman of wounds," it would seem strange if the quoted lines should not pre-eminently and immediately demand a Christian, rather than Herculean, interpretation. In order to give Hercules a certain position in the night sky, Olson was obliged to take "owl-light" as "night" rather than the more correct "dusk," which we can take to be the shrouding of the sun at Christ's death. "Half-way house," according to Olson, is the "autumnal equinox"; but surely the phrase ties up with the "half-way winds" of later in the poem, both symbols of mortality, this-worldliness. The "half-way house" will be the whole transitory world — a halting-place midway between two stages of a journey (see the *OED*). The "furies" are best seen as Christ's earthly passions and sins, which die with Him. He lies "graveward" in the sense that he is making for the grave; also he is in the position of an altar in a church ("altarwise" as defined in the *OED*), the living prototype of our common symbolic cross. In order to explain "altarwise," Olson makes an amazing side-step, discarding altogether his picture of the night sky and substituting an alternative system where Hercules represents the sun "moving southward as the year wears on, in the direction of the contellation Ara, the Altar; hence 'altarwise'" (p. 68). But the suffix *-wise* indicates manner not direction. If Dylan Thomas had ever set himself the fantastic job of laying clues for the expert in astronomy, the meticulousness of mind so required would at least have supplied "altarbound" or "altarward." To take the "gentleman" to be Christ does not make this a simple poem, but it does mean that the ingenuities here are the same kind as we have found in other poems of Thomas'. Were "gentleman" to stand for Hercules, it would be little more than a subterfuge to avoid giving the name; whereas the anonymity of "gentleman" is appropriate for Thomas' "Jack Christ." And further, an ear for Thomas' wordplay will give us "*gentle* man" as an expression of Christ's meekness. For further discussion see Ralph N. Maud, "Dylan Thomas Astro-navigated," *Essays in Criticism*, V (April 1955), 164-168, and Monroe C. Beardsley and Sam Hynes, "Misunderstanding Poetry: Notes on Some Readings of Dylan Thomas," *College English*, XXI (March 1960), 315-322.

CHAPTER V

1. John Malcolm Brinnin, *Dylan Thomas in America* (Boston: Little, Brown, 1955), p. 128; in Brinnin, *Casebook*, p. 208.

2. "Ye shall have a hempen caudle then, and the help of hatchet" — *Henry VI*, pt. 2, IV. vii. 95. When the *OED* records only one other instance of this kind of comic reference to hanging (in the Marprelate Epistles), one is intrigued by the question of where Thomas got the phrase in the first place if not from the *OED* itself. Perhaps he knew his early Shakespeare histories and Marprelate tracts better than one might suppose?

3. "Three Poems," in *QE* (U.S.), pp. 178-180. See also note to *In the white giant's thigh*, *Botteghe oscure*, No. 6 (November 1950), pp. 335-337. *In Country Heaven* (unpublished) is a verse rendering of this prose explanation.

4. R. B. Marriott writes in *Adam International Review*, No. 238 (Dylan Thomas Memorial Number, 1953), p. 31: "In 1935, when first I knew Dylan Thomas, he said: 'I shall be dead within two years.'" In contrast we have Phillip Burton quoting Thomas as saying in 1952: "I've got another twenty, or perhaps twenty-five, years to live. . . ." (*Ibid.*, p. 36). The last poems do not reflect that view.

5. Brinnin, *Dylan Thomas in America*, p. 274:

> Dylan waked and dozed intermittently. "The horrors" were still there, he said — "abstractions, triangles and squares and circles." Once he said to Liz, "You told me you had a friend who had d.t.'s. What was it like?" "He saw white mice and roses," said Liz. "Roses plural?" asked Dylan, "or Rose's roses, with an apostrophe?" Then Liz said, "You know, Dylan, one thing about horrors — just remember, they go away, they do go away —" "Yes," said Dylan, "I believe you." As she sat beside him holding his hand in hers, she suddenly felt his grip stiffen. When she looked at Dylan his face was turning blue. A quick call to Dr. Feltenstein brought an ambulance that took Dylan to St. Vincent's Hospital.

APPENDIX I

1. See "Note" dated November 1952 in *Collected Poems 1934-1952* (London: J. M. Dent & Sons, 1952) and undated in *The Collected Poems of Dylan Thomas* (New York: New Di-

rections, 1953). These two editions differ in pagination but not in the text. The five constituent volumes are *18 Poems* (London: The Sunday Referee and the Parton Bookshop, 1934), *Twenty-five Poems* (London: J. M. Dent & Sons, 1936), *The Map of Love* (London: J. M. Dent & Sons, 1939), *Deaths and Entrances* (London: J. M. Dent & Sons, 1946), *In Country Sleep* (New York: New Directions, 1952). *Paper and Sticks* (in *DE*) was dropped while the *Collected Poems* was in proof. *Once below a time*, not previously included in a volume, was added in *CP*, as was *Author's Prologue*.

2. The four poetry Notebooks at the Lockwood Library are presently being prepared for publication. Manuscripts presented to the British Museum by Trevor Hughes confirm many points and, in the case of *Especially when the October wind*, fill a striking gap. Documents in the Harvard College Library and in the T. E. Hanley collection are also corroborative. Communications concerning like manuscripts or relevant information are solicited. Enquiries may be addressed to the author, Lockwood Library, State University of New York, Buffalo 14, New York.

3. Only three Notebook poems appeared in *Swansea Grammar School Magazine*. *Orpheus* in *SGSM* July 1930 is a traditional pastoral, thoroughly deleted in the 1930 Notebook. *Two Images* in *SGSM* April 1931, dated 28 and 29 December 1930 in Notebook, both prompted the poet's later marginal "Ugh."

4. See also Treece, 2d ed., chap. viii, *passim;* Stanford, pp. 64, 73; W. S. Merwin, "A Religious Poet," *Adam International Review* (1953), p. 75; Randall Swingler, "Recent Verse," *New English Weekly* (1 October 1936), pp. 409-410. The few poems of Thomas' congenial to David Holbrook, dealt with under "The True Voice of Dylan Thomas" in his book *Llareggub Revisited* (Cambridge: Bowes & Bowes, 1962), p. 191, are early ones:

> It would be interesting to know under what circumstances these poems in which a true voice or partly true voice appears — *Should lanterns shine, I have longed to move away* and *Out of the sighs* — were composed. At what points of personal balance was Thomas able to contemplate his predicament with some objectivity. . . . Perhaps the most revealing of the true poems is *O make me a mask.* . . .

The chronology answers the question. These poems cannot be held to reveal valuable moments of self-awareness in the mature Thomas. The "true voice" of Dylan Thomas remains in the long, difficult poems.

5. A tabulated representation of the poetic output appears in Ralph N. Maud, "Dylan Thomas' *Collected Poems:* Chronology of Composition," *PMLA*, LXXVI (June 1961), pp. 292-297.

6. See Tedlock, p. 17; Brinnin, *Casebook*, p. 280.

7. Charles Rare Books, Catalogue Forty-One, lists "Proof of *Twenty-Three Poems* 1936. Advance proof copy in printed drab wrappers, actually *Twenty-five Poems* lacking *And death shall have no dominion* and *Then was my neophyte*, with two versions of *To-day, this insect*, one of which was never published."

8. With reference to the term "exhausters," what Thomas wrote to Vernon Watkins on 13 November 1937 about *The spire cranes* (originally a January 1931 poem) applies equally to his practice for the previous couple of years (*LVW*, p. 31):

> I've done another little poem: nothing at all important, or even (probably) much good: just a curious thought said quickly. I think it will be good for me to write some short poems, not bothering about them too much, between my long exhausters.

What he had done with *The spire cranes* was to regularize and reduce by about half a very free short-lined poem from the 1930-1932 Notebook, retaining the thought and much of the wording. In contrast, the "long exhauster" *Poem to Caitlin* later entitled *I make this in a warring absence* took "roughly a year" to finish; a single line would occupy Thomas for many days (*Ibid.*, p. 30). The difference in tone and achievement between the two poems is great, and immediately apparent. The fact that Thomas was interested in revising early poems is significant in itself; but the main point here is that Thomas' real development as a poet can only be seen by putting to one side the minor strain, the revamped poems, thus isolating his main line of creativity.

9. Watkins coined the engaging term "opossum" to make a contrast with "opus" (*Ibid.*, p. 40). Though Thomas apparently never revealed to his correspondent that these short poems were revisions, he at least put an appropriate value judgment on them. To Henry Treece he frankly explained that he had written the "straight" poems of *25P* "quite a long time before the other poems," and referred to the early notebooks in a letter dated July 1938.

10. This was the period in which Thomas had ambitions for a Jarvis novel. Glyn Jones in "Dylan Thomas — The Other Man," *Western Mail* (21 April 1958) mentions bringing away with him from his first visit to Thomas (about April 1934) "type-script copies of, among others, 'The mouse and the woman,' 'The visitors,' and 'The enemies.'" He also recalls Thomas working on "The Orchards" at that time.

11. Thomas wrote of *To Others than You:* "Here is a new short poem, nothing very much" (*LVW*, p. 68). At least two lines were not new: (1) "Desireless familiar," as Thomas' letter

indicates, came from "The Orchards," and (2) "My friends were enemies on stilts" came from Notebook poem 2 April 1933. The "opossums" apparently continue into *DE. When I Woke* goes back to a February 1933 Notebook poem for its opening line (see also *Ibid.*, p. 41). *The Hunchback in the Park* and *On the Marriage of a Virgin*, published in 1941, were drafted almost ten years earlier.

12. See note 8.

13. *LVW*, p. 39.

14. *Ibid.*, p. 37. Watkins indicates that the fourth poem was the draft of *After the funeral*. The simplest explanation is that five poems, not four, were enclosed, and that Thomas added this unfinished poem without including it in his count.

15. *Ibid.*, p. 40.

16. An indication that *How shall my animal* should be taken as a major effort is that Thomas sent it to *Criterion*, a periodical with "an established snob-appeal," where he had planned to send his previous major poem, the poem to Caitlin (*Ibid.*, pp. 33, 31). That poem, if sent, was rejected; *How shall my animal* was accepted. Place of publication, as we have seen with the revised poems sent to *Poetry*, is generally a good indication of the value Thomas placed on a poem, in turn a guide to how he wrote it, whether easy revision or hard driving.

17. *Ibid.*, pp. 57, 40.

18. The contents of *ML* are divided into two groups in the Chronology. A similar division for *25P* is more difficult. The undisputably "major" poems are *I, in my intricate image, A grief ago, Hold hard, these ancient minutes in the cuckoo's month*, and *Altarwise by owl-light*. The teasers *Now* and *How soon the servant sun* were acknowledged to be in a special category (*Ibid.*, p. 16). *To-day, this insect* was exhaustively rewritten from its early version. *Find meat on bones, Foster the light, Grief thief of time, Do you not father me* might best be considered as part of the major effort that produced *18P*. The suggestion that *Then was my neophyte* is a revised poem is completely conjectural. In December 1936 Thomas considered it the best poem in the book.

19. *Ibid.*, p. 48.

Index of Thomas' Poems

5467